T0299185

Understanding Strategic Analysis

Understanding Strategic Analysis is a concise and practical guide for organisational strategic analysis, strategy development, decision-making, and implementation.

The book takes the reader step by step through the background of strategic management and the process of developing a new strategy. It considers how to assess the strategic capabilities and context of the organisation, how to identify and choose between the various strategic options, and how to successfully implement the change in strategy. Mini-case studies and reflective questions provide stimuli for class discussion, whilst chapter objectives and summaries structure and reinforce learning. The final chapter sets out a complete worked example to illustrate the process as a whole.

Refreshing and concise, this text provides valuable and practical reading for postgraduate, MBA and executive education students of strategic management, as well as practising managers in organisations of all sizes. Online resources include a short Instructor's Manual, chapter-by-chapter PowerPoint slides, and a test bank of exam questions.

Tom Elsworth is Senior Lecturer in Leadership, General Management and Strategic Management at Oxford Brookes University, UK. Previously, he has held posts as Finance Director of OMNI Communications Ltd, a private PR business operating across the EU (2000–2006); Head of PR at Joint European Torus, a Euratom-funded research project (mid-1995–2000); Director of Brussels Marketing Office at AEA Technology (1994–mid-1995); and Company Secretary at Fusion Business, UK Atomic Energy Authority, a UK government-funded research project (1992–1999). He has also held various posts with the UK Atomic Energy Authority both in the US and the UK.

Understanding Strategic Analysis

A Simple Guide to Choosing, Developing and Implementing Business Strategy

Tom Elsworth

Routledge
Taylor & Francis Group

LONDON AND NEW YORK

First published 2024
by Routledge
4 Park Square, Milton Park, Abingdon, Oxon OX14 4RN

and by Routledge
605 Third Avenue, New York, NY 10158

Routledge is an imprint of the Taylor & Francis Group, an informa business

British Library Cataloguing-in-Publication Data
A catalogue record for this book is available from the British Library

ISBN: 978-1-032-38513-6 (hbk)
ISBN: 978-1-032-38511-2 (pbk)
ISBN: 978-1-003-34539-8 (ebk)

DOI: 10.4324/9781003345398

Typeset in Berling
by Apex CoVantage, LLC

Access the Support Material: www.routledge.com/9781032385112

Contents

1   Introduction   1

Deals with the ideas behind the book and recommends ways in which different readers may use it. Points out also what the book is not, a formal academic text, but how it may be used as an adjunct to the classic texts in the role of practical training manual.

2   Strategic management and why it is important   7

Sets the scene around the importance and utility of strategic analysis and distinguishes strategic analysis from the use made of similar techniques at the operational level in fields such as marketing, human resources management (HRM), logistics, and others.

3   The process of developing and implementing a new strategy   12

Gives an overview of the whole strategic process and thereby of the structure of the following main chapters in this book. This chapter lays out all the tools of strategic analysis in the order in which they will be of use. The tools reviewed will be resource audit, VRIO analysis, benchmarking, accounting measures of performance, business definition, Porter's 5 Forces, industry life cycle, strategic groups analysis, critical success factors, PESTEL, SWOT, Porter's generic business strategies, strategy clock, BCG Matrix, Ansoff's Matrix, organic and inorganic growth methods, international strategy types, SAF evaluation of options, stakeholder mapping, force field analysis, Lewin's Three Phase model, and change agency.

Details use of the tools and methods used to analyse the resources and competencies of the existing organisation to establish a clear and objective understanding of its internal strengths and weaknesses.

Covers the use of the tools and methods used to analyse the industry and sector of which our organisation is part of, together with the broader macro-environmental factors impacting the industry. This is done to establish a clear and objective understanding of the drivers of change and hence, the opportunities and threats that our industry faces.

Presents the results of our analysis in a SWOT grid and discusses its uses and abuses. Also demonstrates the extension of SWOT to derive immediate strategic options for organisational growth and improvement.

Covers the use of the idea of generic strategic types to identify suitable long-term strategic stances, considering our current strategic position and our organisational objectives, values, and mission.

Sets out the use of a tool systematically to choose between the strategic options that have been generated.

Deals with the use of the tools and methods to prepare for and then drive the changes required to operationalise the newly chosen strategy.

A detailed case study is presented and analysed showing how all the tools are applied to it with explanations at each step.

Figures

Tables

Acknowledgements

I should like to acknowledge the work of John Mulcahy and David Calfo, my colleagues at Oxford Brookes Business School. They very kindly spent a good deal of time reading through my work, advising me, and suggesting improvements and corrections. Any errors or infelicities remaining are entirely my own fault.

CHAPTER 1

Introduction

INTRODUCTION TO *UNDERSTANDING STRATEGIC ANALYSIS*

Understanding Strategic Analysis is a book on strategic organisational management, designed to provide the student, whether undergraduate or postgraduate or a degree apprentice or a corporate trainee, with a kit of strategic management tools and giving worked examples. It might be thought of in the same vein as a car workshop manual: there are diagrams, words of practical advice about what works and what is problematic, the tools that are applied to an illustrative case, and links that are provided for further reading for those interested.

Minimal prior knowledge is assumed, and *Understanding Strategic Analysis* offers a thorough but focused knowledge of organisational strategic management sufficient to enable a good practical job to be done of developing and implementing a new organisational strategy. It will allow a job of strategic analysis to be done that is easily sufficient to get a good pass in higher education or win the praise of the boss. It will also be very useful to the entrepreneur planning a small start-up and to the busy manager of a small or medium-sized enterprise seeking to understand performance and the options for growth or to respond to changed circumstances. *Understanding Strategic Analysis* is not an academic textbook in the normal sense, but at every stage, it indicates links to areas of underlying academic theory so that those interested may follow up with a much deeper and broader programme of reading.

Many years of teaching experience show that most students studying strategy courses lack practical organisational experience. This is important because, although the fundamental theory in the field is very simple as will be seen on the following pages, it is not easy to apply the theory to practice without practical experience of managing and of the organisation and industry to which the theory is to be applied. This book tackles this problem by adopting the approach of setting out the theory in the form of a series of practical "tools of the trade" and will give nuggets of advice on what works and what does not work in practice. All of this is illustrated diagrammatically and through worked examples. In this way, it intends to demystify and simplify the art of strategic management offering practical ways forward.

HOW TO USE *UNDERSTANDING STRATEGIC ANALYSIS*

It is hoped that the reader will work through their own strategic management project with this book at their side for reference as well as having reviewed the advice it contains before embarking on their own project.

DOI: 10.4324/9781003345398-1

Every main chapter has a case study, taken from a wide variety of contexts, which the reader can use to ensure that they understand the material. The case studies will enable the reader to see how to apply the tools. The case questions can be used in teaching situations, or the individual reader will find them a good route towards testing their understanding and prompting ideas about how to address their own projects.

The chapters are set out, as follows, in a sequence which, from Chapter 4, matches the steps the reader will take in their own project:

Chapter 2 serves to set the scene, seeking to give a clear explanation of what strategic management is all about.

Chapter 3 reviews the whole process of undertaking a strategic analysis of an organisation, from start to finish, providing structure for the chapters following.

Chapter 4 asks the reader to assess their own organisation: what is it good at, and what is it not good at?

Chapter 5 asks the reader to look in detail at the context in which their organisation is placed: what is found there which is threatening, and what is there to be found which offers opportunity?

Chapter 6 seeks to bring together into a single, clear picture the outcome of these preceding analyses and take first steps towards drawing conclusions about what might be done to enhance future organisational effectiveness.

Chapter 7 deals with the ways in which the reader could think about the different types of strategies which may be available to their organisation and will lead to the setting out of a range of possible strategies all of which could be advantageous.

Chapter 8 offers the reader a simple and systematic way to choose between these strategic options.

Chapter 9 then addresses the all-important question of how this choice might be turned into real actions in the organisation that will lead to improved performance.

Chapter 10 is, in effect, an appendix with a special purpose. It is another complete worked example, but of a very different type of organisation facing different challenges, to illustrate the process of conducting an organisational strategic analysis showing in detail how to tackle the job. This final case study is also wholly fictional but closely based on real organisations and circumstances.

THE CHAPTER EXAMPLE CASE – MOTORSPORT ENGINEERING LTD.

The following case (Motorsport Engineering Ltd, or MEL) is intended to offer a helpful, albeit imaginary, context in which readers can base their thinking about the material in this book. The concepts in each chapter are applied to MEL as the penultimate part of the chapter. Readers, either individually or in a class discussion, are encouraged to consider how Sarah, our imaginary strategist, set about undertaking the task of applying material from that chapter to her company. The worked example case is then followed in each chapter by a special chapter case for class discussion.

Please read the MEL case before commencing the following chapters.

BACKGROUND TO THE CASE

MEL is a private limited company that manufactures high-performance fixing components (bolts, nuts, washers, etc.) with a special focus on the motorsport, defence, and offshore oil sectors. It was established in 1990 by three engineers who were made redundant when the Jaguar brand was bought by Ford in 1989.

MEL has a hard-earned reputation, now maintained for more than 30 years, for keeping up with the latest technology in their field and for producing the highest quality goods delivered on time. It has grown gradually to more than 300 employees working in administration, purchasing, marketing, design, production, and customer service departments. All are in one large building located in an industrial park in Oxfordshire near to both the M4 and the M40, giving access to the wider road system in the UK. The building is not new but was refurbished soon after the company was established following early success and swift growth almost to its current size. This early success was built around its original key customer group built on the Formula 1 teams located in Oxfordshire and neighbouring counties in England. This group of customers remains MEL's most important. The founders attribute their success to their values as innovative engineers, expressed in the company mission "keeping up to date keeps us well ahead of the rest". This is reflected in well-established systems to ensure continuous improvement as part of a first-class Total Quality Management system. An innovative approach to manufacturing systems, as well as to products, has allowed MEL successfully to grow, despite the highly competitive nature of all its markets, by providing often urgent, on-time deliveries to its very demanding customer base.

Staff are generally rewarded near the top of the range for the industry and staff turnover is low with many employees able to recall the early years of the business. The internal communications processes at MEL are sophisticated with a strong culture of worker participation. Management and employees are firmly linked to the broader customer network via regular customer feedback briefings.

Equally, suppliers are closely integrated into the MEL systems via regular onsite discussions. MEL and their suppliers work in a closely coordinated fashion focused on meeting the precise needs of their customers.

The original leadership team remains in charge, with the later additions of Tim Jones and Jeff Castle, although other investors have by now greatly diluted their ownership. These investors are individuals, well known to Tim Jones and Jeff Castle from within the broader automotive industry and from among the Motorsport fanbase. There is no dominant shareholder. The Management Team, each of whom owns 5% of the company shares, consists of the following:

John Smith, Managing Director

Tim Jones, Finance Director

Joe Coles, Engineering and Production Director

Jeff Castle, Marketing and Sales Director

Martin Summers, Company Secretary and Administration Director

MEL is regarded in the industry as a very well-run and successful organisation. However, recent financial performance has been giving the Management Team serious cause for concern. The following accounts were presented by Martin Summers at a meeting of the Management Team in late 2021. Pre-pandemic figures were presented to avoid drawing conclusions from the special circumstances of 2020, Martin said that he expected the final 2021 figures to be essentially the same as those for 2019.

Key Financial Data	2019 £M	2018 £M	2017 £M
Turnover	15	19	18
Profit (loss) before taxation	2.5	4.6	4.5
Net assets (liab.)	6	7	7
Shareholders' funds	5.9	6.9	6.5
Profit margin	17%	24%	25%
Return on capital employed	41%	65%	67%

Cash Flow	2019 £M	2018 £M	2017 £M
Cash in (out) flow operational, activities	3.4	4.9	3.6
Taxation	−0.149	−0.7	−0.5
Capital expenditure & financial investments		−0.2	−0.2
Equity dividends paid	−3.5	−3.8	−3.6
Increase (decrease) cash & equivalent	**−0.25**	**0.2**	**−0.7**

Balance Sheet	2019 £M	2018 £M	2017 £M
Land & buildings	1.1	1.1	1.2
Plant & vehicles	.4	.5	.5
Fixed Assets	**1.5**	**1.6**	**1.7**

Balance Sheet	2019 £M	2018 £M	2017 £M
Stock & W.I.P.	2.2	2.5	2.2
Trade debtors	1.3	1.3	1.9
Bank & deposits	1.7	1.8	1.5
Other current assets	.29	.32	.3
Other debtors	.12	.17	.16
Prepayments	.1	.13	.14
Deferred taxation	.068	.015	
Current assets	**5.8**	**6.2**	**6.2**
Trade creditors	−0.5	−0.38	−0.38
Short-term loans & overdrafts	−.028		
Bank overdrafts	−.028		
Corporation tax			−.27
Total other current liabilities	−0.34	-0.15	−0.62
Current liabilities	**−0.89**	**−0.53**	**−1.27**
Long-term debt	−.065		
Provisions for other liab.	−058	−058	−040
Long-term liabilities	**−123**	**−058**	**−040**
Net assets	**5.9**	**6.9**	**6.5**

Jeff Castle then tabled the following very worrying marketing information.

KEY MARKET PERFORMANCE INDICATORS

Key Performance Indicators	2019	2018	2017
Customer satisfaction	83%	93%	95%
Motorsport market share	25%	28%	30%

The customer satisfaction data were particularly shocking to the Management Team. They had not been aware of this area of concern at all. Jeff said that he had the data from his team just the day before; previously, he had heard some rumblings but nothing to this degree. His team had told him that it seemed to them that the main area of customer concern was around MEL's ability quickly to design and supply bespoke fittings for the Motorsport customers. These were at the very core of the MEL business; John, Joe, and Martin wondered aloud whether they were beginning to lose touch with the operational realities of the organisation.

The Management Team concluded that they were right to be concerned as performance generally appeared to be drifting downwards. They felt that these results were not in keeping with performance expectations in their industry as a whole or in the sectors they served.

The Management Team also discussed the significant changes in the automotive industry amid the move to electric vehicles (EVs), a change that was already happening fast and seen to be accelerating. The challenge of this change was greater for the component makers than for the car manufacturers themselves. The latter were still making cars, but, for example, an engine manufacturer faced a complete loss of its market. Jeff Castle reported that the big, internal combustion–focused component companies such as BorgWarner appeared to be opting for a strategy of acquisition to transform themselves into EV suppliers. It was reported that they planned for 5% of sales to be EV-related in 2022, 25% of sales by 2025 and 45% by 2030 – just 9 years away! Arguably the situation for MEL and its direct competitors making engineered components such as fixings is not quite so dramatic, and there are also suppliers of electrical equipment to the automotive industry which may be able to accommodate the new reality with relatively small change. But the team also noted that the Motorsport market was also under pressure, from several directions, to move in the direction of EVs, and a Formula E had existed now for several years.

The team concluded that the time was more than ripe for a thorough review of the strategic position. Jeff Castle was asked to supervise the project and he appointed a member of his team, Sarah Riley, Head of CRM, to be the project manager. The Management Team asked for a detailed report with recommendations in 3 months. They needed to renew their understanding of what was happening in MEL and what their strategic options were.

CHAPTER 2

Strategic management and why it is important

WHAT IS STRATEGY, AND WHY IS IT IMPORTANT?

Strategy has been defined simply as "the long-term direction of the organisation".[1] Strategic management is the process by which we decide upon and implement our strategy.

We can never know everything that there is to know, even about our own organisation, and what there is to know is in a state of continuous change, so strategising is about making decisions in situations of uncertainty. The decisions made will have major impacts on the organisation and on outside relationships such as with suppliers and customers. They are the decisions which will drive significant change, change which will radically impact the lives of employees and other stakeholders. The decisions we make will also be very complex in terms of both the decision-making process, the main focus of this book, and in terms of the nature of the impact of the decision on all the elements that make up the organisation and its context.

Our approach to the strategic process

There are two equally valid ways of thinking about strategy: the rational or planning approach and the emergent approach. In this context, strategy has been described as both "a plan" and "a pattern of consistent behaviour".[2] This manual adopts a rational strategy approach for the main part while recognising that unplanned organisational change is occurring all the time as people take action to deal with their everyday experiences (see Chapter 9 especially on this). Our rational approach assumes the following:

- Organisational influences need careful analysis using well-developed and proven tools (see Chapter 3).
- Organisational strengths and resources have to be harnessed to enable the exploitation of external opportunities and dealing with threats (see Chapter 4).
- Strategic analysis follows this and then informs the actions taken (see Chapters 5, 6, and 7).

DOI: 10.4324/9781003345398-2

- Logical conclusions that are evidence-based will be reached and the system can be controlled by careful assessment of feedback from the outcome of the decisions made (see Chapters 8 and 9).
- Thus, the organisation can hope to deliver its overall mission and purpose (see Chapter 3).

FUNCTIONAL, BUSINESS, AND CORPORATE LEVELS OF STRATEGY

To help cope with the complexity, the whole process of strategising is thought of normally in terms of three levels (see Figure 2.1):

- **Corporate-Level Strategy** – concerned with the overall purpose and scope of an organisation and how value will be added to the different parts (business units) of the organisation. It answers the question, "What businesses should we be in?"
- **Business Unit Strategy** – about how to compete successfully in particular markets. It answers the question, "How do we best conduct the business we are in?" or "How do we gain a competitive advantage?"
- **Functional or Operational Strategy** – concerned with how the component parts of the organisation, for example, the marketing department or the human resources management department, deliver business unit and corporate strategies effectively. It

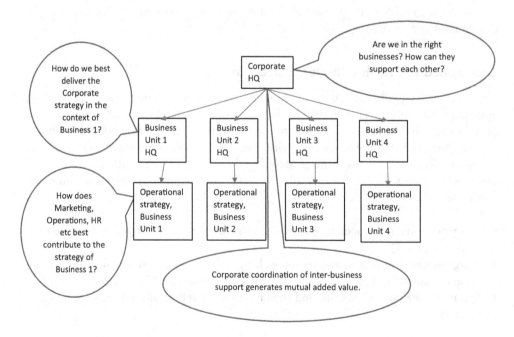

FIGURE 2.1 Levels of strategy in a generic corporate organisation

answers the question, "How does my department best contribute to the organisational business and corporate strategy?"

The purpose of all these levels of strategy together is to deliver the overall organisational mission. This mission might often be commercial in nature but also often will be governmental, social, or charitable. In the broadest terms then, the mission is not only to create value and financial certainty but also societal value for the stakeholders of the organisation (e.g. including owners, customers, clients, service users, suppliers, employees, etc.). But if this delivery is to be successful, then it is important to check that the strategy implemented at a lower level is consistent with and contained within the strategy implemented at a higher level. This is easier said than done, especially in a larger organisation that is beyond the scope of individual oversight. The usual approach to this is carefully to set, monitor, review and regularly revise operational and business unit targets.

CHAPTER CASE – TESLA

Tesla mini case

Tesla Motors designs, develops, manufactures, and sells fully electric vehicles (EVs). It sells products directly to customers through retail locations and the company's website. It has operations across North America, Europe, and Asia. It offers four models of car, ranging from a compact model to a full-sized SUV. Revenues from car sales account for the vast majority of the company's income.

Tesla Motors has been called "the world's most important automotive company" and Tesla's Model S, "the Most Loved Vehicle in America" – outselling the Mercedes S-class and the BMW 7 series. How can Tesla Motors be so successful after so many years of poor performance by US car companies?

A key part of the story is technological; lithium-ion batteries were improving dramatically in performance. Equally, the founders, who had no experience making cars, realised that car companies now outsourced everything, even styling. Production of the Tesla Roadster began in 2008.

Tesla's strategy is to succeed in the high end of the market, where customers will pay a premium for a sports car, and then move down the market rapidly to higher volumes and lower prices with each successive model. All free cash flow is ploughed back into research and development (R&D) to drive down costs and bring follow-on products to market as fast as possible.

Tesla's mission statement says that the company's goal is to "accelerate the world's transition to sustainable energy". Tesla's vision is "to build the most compelling automobile company of the 21st century by spearheading the world's transition to EVs".

Tesla's innovation speed in the high-end automobile industry is comparable to Google or Amazon rather than other car manufacturers; its increasing market value is a clear signal that, to survive, the other car firms will be required to develop more inventive, Tesla-like business models. Tesla has surpassed Volkswagen to become the world's second-most valuable vehicle business behind Toyota with a market capitalization that is greater than that of Ford and GM combined. Tesla sales volumes grew by almost three quarters in 2022 compared with 2021. The firm had reported a record profit in 2021.

Tesla is fully aligned to the cause of minimising global warming. Who would not want to possess a car that does not pollute the environment, does not require trips to refuel, and is genuinely green?

Tesla has empowered customers by simplifying the buying process to one of direct online purchase. Tesla does not follow a traditional advertisement strategy of advertising in leading newspapers or advertising on television or radio; instead, it assumes that customers are clever and would seek them out.

EVs are far less complicated than their internal combustion counterparts. They contain many fewer components per vehicle. The total cost of ownership for customers is substantially reduced because of this simplicity.

However, Tesla also faces all the normal everyday difficulties. For example, although it expects to deliver about 50% more vehicles in 2022 than in 2020, like other carmakers, it is struggling with a post-pandemic shortage of computer chips.

It is also persisting with its original plan to build a zero-emission energy business. The intention is to produce many times more batteries than their nearest EV competitor. Besides bringing the cost of cars down to affordable small car prices the batteries will also go towards Tesla's home–energy–storage business. That would create what it calls a "giant distributed utility" that can cope with increased electricity demand as more people use EVs.

Sources: MarketLine Company Profile December 2021, P. Regner, G. Johnson, & K. Scholes (2019). Exploring Strategy Text and Cases, Pearson, Tesla Delivers Record Number of Cars Despite Challenges, BBC News 04/05/2022, The Magical Realism of Tesla, The Economist 30/05/2022

Tesla case class discussion questions

1. Why has Tesla been so successful?
2. Identify concepts discussed in this chapter which are evident in the Tesla case.

Suggested class activities

1. Identify an organisation that a member of the class knows well, perhaps they work there, or they did in the past or perhaps it is their family firm. Divide the class into small groups and invite them, separately, to interview the class member, say, for 5 minutes. They should then work together to develop a presentation in which they describe the overall

purpose of the organisation and identify examples of the operational-, business-, and, if appropriate, corporate-level activities of the organisation, showing how they are linked. An alternative version of this activity is for the tutor to be the interviewee and use the HE institution as the organisation.

2. Divide the class into small groups. Ask each group to present their solution to one of the following questions. The groups should be allowed 30 minutes to conduct desk research. In each case, the group should try to say why the steps were taken and categorise the activity in the terms set out in this chapter:

- Identify at least one example of an organisation which acquired or merged with another organisation in a different industry.
- Identify at least one example of an organisation which sold or closed one of its business units.
- Identify at least one example of an organisation which launched a new product or service that is based on a completely new technological solution.
- Identify at least one example of an organisation which reorganised and consolidated operations into fewer separate entities.

NOTES

1 Whittington, R., Regnér, P., Angwin, D., Johnson, G. & Scholes, K. *Exploring Strategy*, 12th Edn, Harlow: Pearson, 2020

2 Mintzberg, H. *Tracking Strategies: Towards a General Theory*, Oxford: Oxford University Press, 2007

CHAPTER 3

The process of developing and implementing a new strategy

TYPICAL ELEMENTS OF A STRATEGY PROJECT

The projects we undertake will always consist of these steps (see Figure 3.1), each of which can be seen in the worked example case study (Chapter 10).

The references in this diagram to internal and external analysis are crucial to the structure of the process of strategic analysis. The meaning of these terms can best be understood from the following diagram (see Figure 3.2), demonstrating the overall position of the organisation within the wider economic and socio-political world.

INTERNAL CONTEXT

Some analysts start with the furthest external context and work inwards towards the organisation itself, but experience shows that the most difficult and time-consuming task is to form a really clear and accurate view our own organisation – its purpose, its resources, its capabilities, and its performance. We should start therefore with this difficult part of the project.

The **purpose** of the organisation, which is the fundamental driver of the strategy we adopt, is intended to help us achieve our overall, long-term wishes, that is, our **mission** and **vision**. It is a good idea to encapsulate these in a published statement so that everyone involved in the organisation plus wider stakeholders, such as customers and suppliers, all have a common understanding of what the organisation is there to do and how it will do it.

An outline of such a strategy statement could be to give:

- The basic goals of the organisation,
- The scope of the organisation's activities, and
- The means or capabilities on which the organisation's activities depend.

In this way, we can set the scene for our strategising, providing clarity and direction to our thinking.

DOI: 10.4324/9781003345398-3

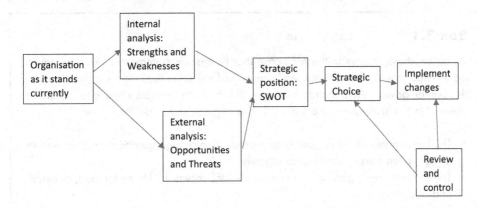

FIGURE 3.1 An idealised view of the process of strategic analysis

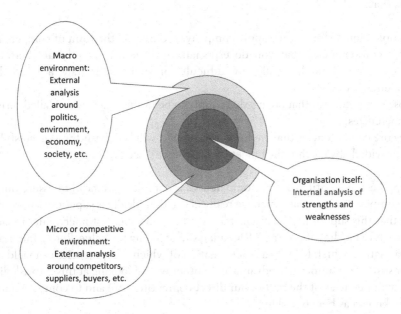

FIGURE 3.2 The internal, competitive, and macro environments of the organisation

The obvious next questions to ask are, How shall we be able to do this? What means or capabilities do we actually have, and how useful will they be? The approach to answering this question starts with conducting a **resources audit**. In using this

---

Box 3.1 Setting the Scene at MEL

As an example, it says in the MEL case that its mission statement is "keeping up to date keeps us well ahead of the rest". This would not seem really to be sufficient given the earlier advice. As it stands it is more like a motto encapsulating one important element in the historical success of MEL. We might wish to add the following:

- The basic goals of the organisation – production of high-specification engineering fixings, often bespoke and often urgently.
- The scope of the organisation's activities – MEL serves the UK motorsport, defence, and offshore sectors.
- The means or capabilities on which the organisation's activities depend – highest quality design and production to minimum timescales.

---

approach, we are applying the so-called **resource-based view of strategy**.[1] In brief, this contends that:

- To implement a strategy, we apply company resources in the form of **competencies**.
- Those competencies that you do especially well and, hopefully, are better than the competitor's and, ideally, are difficult for them to imitate are called **core competencies**.
- Those competencies that are needed simply to be in the industry are called **threshold competencies**.
- The core competencies that we have or can build will be a basis for a successful strategy provided always that they meet the customer's needs.

But the process of identifying core competences is complex. We need to assure ourselves that the competency is one at which we really excel, that ideally is superior to the competitor, and that this superiority is sustainable over time and the customer values its output. An approach to tackling this is the **VRIO analysis**,[2] standing for Value, Rarity, Inimitability, and Organisation, which leads to a determination of which competencies can yield a temporary or sustained competitive advantage. Another way of looking at this is to ask directly what the competences of the best of our direct competitors are and to compare ourselves with that, known as **benchmarking**.

Finally, in this assessment of strategic capabilities we should look at the current performance of our organisation asking if it is improving or otherwise and how it compares in this with norms in our industry, we do this using **accounting measures of performance**.

All this internal analysis is brought together into an overall understanding of our internal strategic position in terms of **strengths and weaknesses**, that is, the things we are good at and which can possibly generate sustainable competitive advantage and the things we are not good at and which therefore might threaten our existing level of competitive advantage.

EXTERNAL CONTEXT

Moving outside our own organisation we look next at the situation of the industry of which we are part, a stage often called **industry analysis.** It is also known as **analysis of the competitive environment** and **analysis of the micro-economic environment.**

The fundamental and most important question here is to define our industry with clarity and accuracy; else, there is a real danger of overlooking significant strategic issues because we falsely consider them to be outside our purview. Too narrow a definition may overlook important competitors. Too wide a definition runs the risk that the analysis we do will become meaningless. Also, industries often are made up of different markets, for example, different geographies or different product or service types which should be analysed separately for similar reasons. Having defined the industry in which we are interested we can use a tool called **Porter's 5 Forces,**[3] which shows us what are the strengths of the forces creating competition in the industry. This will give us clues as to what we need to do to compete successfully and whether the industry is likely to be one which can become profitable. Conducting a **strategic groups analysis** of our industry will identify other organisations which have the same or similar business model to ourselves and any other organisations which form a business model group but of which we are not part. From this, we can think out how to react to and overcome our most direct competitors, and we can also consider whether it might make sense to join a different strategic group by changing our business model.

Industries have **life cycles**; they are born, grow, mature, and die. The ways in which we can run an organisation successfully vary as the industry passes through this life cycle. The type of strategy which we can adopt will change, as will the **critical success factors in the industry**, that is those things which we need to be good at to have any chance of competing successfully.

Having conducted an industry analysis, we must recognise that our industry sits within a wider economic and socio-political world. This is often known as the field of **macroeconomic analysis** and is generally addressed using a tool, variously named but here called **PESTEL, standing for Politics, Economics, Society, Technology, Ecology and Law.** This is a checklist which we can use to make sure we think of all the factors which are of relevance to our industry.

The PESTEL factors can drive change in our industry, often long term but sometimes very swiftly, that we can do little or nothing about. Similarly, factors in our industry will drive change in our own organisation, long and medium term, which we can, to some extent, resist or accommodate ourselves to but which again may be beyond our strength to resist. Taken together, those factors amongst these that will have a major impact are known as **key drivers of change.** Those of these drivers which are positive for the future performance of the industry are called **opportunities**, and those which are negative are termed **threats.**

ASSESSING AND ACTING ON THE STRATEGIC POSITION

The next step is to bring together our internal and external analysis into a single statement of strategic position called a **SWOT**, standing for Strengths, Weaknesses, Opportunities, and Threats. This is used as a simple, clear position statement from which we can understand where we are and what might happen if we make no changes to our activities. Hence, it is a crucial basis for considering what our strategy should be going forward, seeking to use our strengths or build improved strengths, take advantage of opportunities, and avoid threats. We need also to about think how we can amend weaknesses so that we are not exposed thereby to the threats we have identified.

IDENTIFYING STRATEGIC OPTIONS

In addition to thinking through the implications of our SWOT, we might ask what types of strategies exist. We might ask if there are any standard approaches to business strategy that we may successfully be able to deploy to our benefit.

At the level of corporate strategy, that is thinking about which business areas we should be competing in, we can use tools such as the **BCG Matrix,**[4] which helps us to understand how the set of businesses we currently own contribute to overall cash generation and **Ansoff's Matrix**[5] which addresses in what ways we might develop our markets and products and services.

At the level of business strategy, that is thinking about how more effectively to compete in the business we are currently in, we can use tools such as **Porter's Generic Strategies**[6] or the **strategy clock**[7] which address issues such as how to compete, in which parts of our market to compete and what type of value for money offer we should make to our customers.

At both these levels, we will generally need to answer questions about how we can grow our organisation and consider both **organic growth**, using our own existing resources and capabilities, and **inorganic growth**, using some form of alliance, partnership, merger, or purchase of another organisation. It is likely also that even a small organisation in our globalised world may consider a range of approaches to **international strategy** to generate growth.

CHOOSING BETWEEN THE STRATEGIC OPTIONS

Typically, all this analysis and thinking about different types of strategy will throw up a range of options, and we must select one of these to take forward. We must do this in a systematic way, evaluating each in turn and comparing the likely consequences of adopting each. A tool often known as **SAF,**[8] standing for Suitability, Acceptability, and Feasibility is used for this purpose.

Successfully implementing a strategy

All the strategic analysis in the world is of no use if the strategy we come up with is not successfully implemented. As we have seen, strategic change is complex and likely to have a major impact on the operations of the organisation. It will require significant investment and a significant amount of time and, most particularly, will cause the daily lives and short-, medium-, and long-term activities and career prospects of employees to change. All of this is very difficult and fraught with the risk of unexpected outcomes and unfulfilled hopes and plans. Even when everything goes well, the world outside the organisation does not stand still waiting for all this change to be completed. It moves on, perhaps in unexpected directions and at an unanticipated speed. There is an area of management expertise that specialises in this process of implementing new strategies called the **management of change**. Key tools of the change manager, discussed in Chapter 9, include **stakeholder mapping**, understanding the points of view and influence of all our stakeholders; **Lewin's Force Field Analysis**,[9] identifying and evaluating the forces in favour of the change in hand and those opposed; **Lewin's Three Phase Model**, used as a structure for managing the change process; and **change agency**, the identification and deployment of people to help successfully to implement the change.

Conditions for ongoing success

This is a very brief and inadequate description of a complicated process. It will be detailed in subsequent chapters, but it is important to notice here that the process itself is not linear even though it has just been described in that way. The external and internal environments are a ferment of continuous change driven by all sorts of forces beyond the power of the organisation; hence, our analysis and the conclusions we draw from it need to be continuously updated. This is the case even while we are in the mid-analysis, so the process must itself be open and iterative rather than closed and linear. Of course, it is also the case that for the longer term, we must continuously be scanning the internal and external contexts so as not to be caught unawares by change.

It is also important to notice that the analytical process will delve into the depths of the organisation, possibly turning up difficult realities and producing alarming results. It is important to be objective in so far as is possible, to be fearless in facing up to reality, but of course, the whole thing will fail if not backed up by the support and involvement of the highest levels in the organisation.

Box 3.2 Sources of information for strategists

Analysis of organisational resources, capabilities, and performance – Chapter 4

First, it is quite likely that you know your own organisation as well if not better than anyone else. Having said that, you will have colleagues who have specialist knowledge of the various aspects of the organisation and may well also be more experienced than you are yourself. Particularly useful colleagues will be those with a good depth of experience in the organisation but who have also worked in other organisations in the same sector and so can draw comparisons outside the organisation. You will need to be able to access all the organisation's operational and financial information, and to this end, it is essential that the strategic analysis project enjoys active support at the highest levels of the organisation. It is essential that all information garnered is as objective as possible; challenge and seek evidence to support any opinions you are offered; do not take anything as certain or even probable if you are not able to find other internal sources saying the same thing. Specific areas to investigate are listed in Chapter 4.

Analysis of the external context of the organisation – Chapter 5

The competitive environment

If you want to know about your competitors and their products, then ask your Sales Team. They will likely also be the first to know about new entrants to your industry. Substitute products are a more difficult challenge perhaps requiring some imagination fully to conceptualise, but the marketing specialists should have a clear picture of their customers, their needs, and how they can be met. If you want to know about your suppliers, then ask your Purchasing Team. A more general picture of the full range of competitors in your industry and how they fall into groups sharing the same business model (strategic groups) will come from discussions with experienced colleagues combined with an awareness of the industry. This will come from your own experience together with gathering views from the industry (e.g. relevant market intelligence reports from organisations such as Mintel) and professional and business news publications, including *The Times*, *The Financial Times*, *The Economist*, BBC News, or the appropriate newspaper of record for other countries (a newspaper of record is a major national newspaper with large circulation the editorial and newsgathering functions of which are considered authoritative and independent, hence credible, e.g. *Le Monde* in France).

The macro environment

For information about the broader world of society, politics, economics, and so on, you will likely turn principally to the same news sources just mentioned in the previous paragraph. Information on relevant technological and legal developments is to be found in the same sources, but a more focused information base will be accrued from professional and industry-specific sources.

LEGO

Lego AS designs, manufactures, and markets a wide range of toys and games under the LEGO brand name. LEGO operates in Europe, the US, Australia, and Asia. The company is headquartered in Billund, Denmark, and employs about 10,000 people.

In 2000, after 68 years of successful operations, LEGO made its first major loss. It was approaching bankruptcy. Many of LEGO's products were unprofitable or had failed.

In 2004, the Lego Group reached its lowest point as sales dropped by a third in 2003 from 2002. Profit margins fell by a third in the 4 years to 2004. It was not until 2008 that the situation was recovered, and revenue again reached the levels of 1999. In that year, despite shrinkage of the overall market, LEGO's revenues and profits were, up very significantly. How was this turnaround achieved?

The financial situation resulted in a major organisational change, for the first time in its history the group was to be led by a CEO from outside the Kristiansen (formerly spelt Christiansen) family – the family of the original creator: ole Kirk Christiansen. This was not just symbolic; the new CEO Jørgen Vig Knudstorp, was a former management consultant who had joined the board in 2001 to be the director of strategic development. He was a professional manager and had clear ideas about success and good business practices. He took over in 2004 with a clear mandate for change.

When Knudstorp joined LEGO, he found that there were major operational problems and a culture which lacked the ability to tackle them:

- Operations were run unsystematically; for example orders were dealt with largely ad hoc leading to a lot of spare capacity.
- Just a few tens of products were responsible for the vast majority of sales whereas the total catalogue ran to thousands of products.
- Product development of the traditional toy ranges was simply the multiplication of options whereas they had invested heavily in the manufacturing, promotion, and distribution of Lego video games and Lego computer software. These investments had not been a success.
- The list of suppliers, providing for its wide range of individual plastic products, ran to tens of thousands of different companies.
- LEGO managed its customer relations haphazardly spending as much time on smaller toy stores which generated a small percentage of sales as they did on large ones which generated the majority of sales.
- The distribution model was out of date, belonging to an era when customer stores were all small and independent.

The steps Knudstorp started to take had a profound impact on both sales and costs by making efficiency savings so that cash flow moved to be positive by the end of 2005. This allowed an investment to be made in parts of the business which needed it in accordance with his new strategy. For example:

- It closed separate plants in Denmark, France, and Germany, consolidating supply within one plant in the Czech Republic.
- In the US, the group moved supply from an American plant to one in Mexico.
- A list of two dozen different logistics providers was cut to just four, greatly reducing the work needed just to keep logistics running.

It has been said that one of the causes of the fall in revenues was LEGO decision-makers being negatively affected by the notion of markets moving to a fully digital age, hence the failed decision to focus on digital products. This happened even though over two thirds of the company's revenues came from the selling of plastic bricks. Certainly, it is the case that the LEGO turnaround involved selling plastic bricks.

LEGO, the family business, had a culture which seemed indifferent to the bottom line of profit. The business was perhaps too large to be governed, as a family business, by special or narrow interests. But LEGO is a good example of the power of strong leadership and what exactly can be achieved in the space of a few years with willpower and a mandate.

Sources: Innovating a Turnaround at LEGO, HBR Sept 2009, The LEGO group case study, Marketline Feb 2013, LEGO Company Profile, Marketline, March 2022

CASE DISCUSSION QUESTIONS

1. If you were advising Knudstrop, what process of strategic analysis would you follow? How, practically, do you think you would set about that task?
2. From the information in the case, what strengths and weaknesses would be likely to appear in the SWOT you produced?

NOTES

1 Barney, J. Firm Resources and Sustained Competitive Advantage, *Journal of Management*, vol. 17, no. 1 (1991)
2 Whittington, R., Regnér, P., Angwin, D., Johnson, G. & Scholes, K. *Exploring Strategy*, 12th Edn, Harlow: Pearson, 2021

3   Porter, M. The Five Competitive Forces That Shape Strategy, *Harvard Business Review*, vol. 86, no. 1 (2008)

4   Henderson, B. *Henderson on Corporate Strategy*, Cambridge: ABT Books, 1979

5   Ansoff, H. *Corporate Strategy*, London: Penguin, 1988

6   Porter, M. *Competitive Advantage: Creating and Sustaining Superior Performance*, New York: The Free Press, 1985

7   Faulkner, D. & Bowman, C. *The Essence of Competitive Strategy*, London: Prentice Hall, 1995

8   Whittington, R., Regnér, P., Angwin, D., Johnson, G. & Scholes, K. *Exploring Strategy*, 12th Edn, Harlow: Pearson, 2021

9   Lewin, K. *Field Theory in Social Science*, New York: Harper & Row, 1947

CHAPTER 4

Assessing strategic capabilities

THE RESOURCE-BASED VIEW OF STRATEGY

The **resource-based view of strategy**[1] tells us that to implement a strategy we apply company resources in the form of **competencies**. Then, whichever of those competencies that are better than the competitor's and are difficult for them to imitate are called **core competencies**. There are then also those competencies that are needed simply to be in the industry, and these are called **threshold competencies**. So, we see that the core competencies that we have already or can build in some way will be a basis for a successful strategy. It is important to note that core competencies must be involved in the processes and activities that are fundamental to the delivery of **critical success factors** (see Chapter 5).

It is perhaps helpful to set down some definitions of these terms in order to ensure the greatest clarity (always valuable in a strategic analysis as it is such a complex process):

- **Resources** – things we own or can access with which our product or service can be made, marketed, delivered and supported.
- **Competencies** – a linked set of skills, activities and resources enabling us to undertake an organisational task.
- **Threshold Competencies** – those competencies required in order to be able to operate in a particular sector.
- **Core Competencies** – a competency which is the basis for sustainable competitive advantage.
- **Critical Success Factors** – a critical factor or activity required, by the structure of the industry and the needs of customers, to ensure the success of a company or an organisation.

RESOURCES AUDITING

Our first step will be to investigate our resources in detail so that we know clearly what resources we have and how useful they are. This is the process of conducting a **resource audit**. To be sure not to omit any resources, identify them all using the following checklist of resource types.

DOI: 10.4324/9781003345398-4

Type of Resource	Actual Resources – A List of All the Things We Use	Competencies – A Related List of All the Things We Do
Physical	Machines, buildings, raw materials, etc.	Production of outputs desired by customers at a price they will pay
Human	Managers, employees, partners, suppliers, customers	Application of creativity, skills, experience, knowledge, relationships, and motivation to all the processes of the organisation
Financial	Cash flow, capital, assets	Ability to raise funds and apply cash to all the processes of the organisation
Intellectual	Patents, reputation, brands, trademarks	Protects from imitation and builds and protects processes and organisational value and relationships with customers

Then, from that list take each in turn and ask:

- **How much of the resource is really available, and is it of suitable quality/condition?** – For example assets on an asset register may be semi-obsolete, staff may be under-motivated and over-worked, factories and equipment may be ill maintained, suppliers may fail to supply, and the like.
- **Is it unique/providing a competitive advantage?** – Cutting-edge machinery will soon be copied, patents will expire, employees' specialist knowledge will become dated – most of what is unique now will be threshold or, indeed, become useless in the future.

Box 4.1 The Need for Objectivity

Some of these questions are rather difficult and may cause upset and concern among colleagues. The fact-finding involved must therefore be pursued with care, but it is essential that the truth is unearthed.

Resources are of course, of *no value* unless organised into routines and systems, **competencies**, which are the mechanism for the ultimate creation of products or services which will be valued by the final customer. We must ask ourselves how well this process of organisation into routines and systems works in our organisation. Michael Porter developed a very useful model to help with this step of our analysis which he called the **value chain**.[2]

His idea is that an organisation can be thought of as a chain of activities for transforming inputs into outputs and adding value along the way. A key part of the value chain is the linkages between the activities as well as the activities themselves. In Porter's model, the whole chain involves a number of primary and support activities.

Primary activities – directly concerned with the creation or delivery of a product or service:

- Inbound logistics – receiving, storing, and handling raw materials.
- Operations – converting the raw inputs into the finished goods or services.
- Outbound logistics – storing, distributing, and delivering finished goods and services to the customer.
- Marketing and sales – pricing, advertising, and promoting the product.
- Service – all activities that occur after the point of sale to maintain/enhance value.

Support activities – help to improve the effectiveness or efficiency of the primary activities. In this digital age, support activities play an ever more critical role in creating and sustaining competitive advantage:

- Procurement – the processes used to acquire the resource inputs needed for all primary activities.
- Technology – may be directly related to the product or to processes or with a particular resource.
- Human resources management – from recruitment through training and development to reward systems.
- Infrastructure – leadership, culture and structure, finance, planning, and control systems.

By analysing the value chain of our organisation, we can discover where and how value is created or lost within it. It is necessary to consider in detail each of the activity groups listed earlier and ascertain if, how, and how well it contributes to adding value.

Having discovered and evaluated the resources we have and how and how well they are deployed our focus can be narrowed to asking what the bases of our strategic capability are. Do we have:

- **Threshold resources**, that is those that we absolutely need to operate?
- **Unique resources**, that is that are better than our competitors and are difficult for them to imitate?

Does our value chain result in us having:

- **Threshold competencies** enabling us to do the basics demanded by the market?
- **Core competencies** that are better than our competitors and are difficult to imitate and create products or services that are especially valued by customers?

It is essential to focus, during this whole process of analysis, on *value to customers* rather than on what we, internally, may feel is right or appropriate or good or comfortable. In other words, we must strive to be objective and recognise that the organisation exists to serve its customers and only thereby to preserve itself. This is very important, and where many companies get this process wrong, they tend to believe their own rhetoric rather than what the market is telling them.

EVALUATING COMPETENCIES

How then do we seek to ensure that what we believe to be core competencies really are such? What is needed is a method to evaluate our competencies. The one proposed here is called **VRIO analysis**.[3]

The analytical process is to take each suspected core competence in turn and evaluate its **Value, Rarity, Inimitability and Organisational Support**:

V – Value of competencies, in the form of products or services, to customers and in helping us deal with external threats

Does this competency allow us:

- Provide value to customers *but at* a *cost* to us that still allows us to make an acceptable return?
- To take advantage of **opportunities** and neutralise **threats**?

R – Rarity, also possessed by few competitors

Is this competency:

- Possessed uniquely by our own organisation or only by a few others, for example a company may have patented products, supremely talented people, or a powerful brand?
- But only if not rare on a temporary basis, for example patents expire, key individuals can leave or brands can be devalued by adverse publicity?

I – Inimitability, difficult and costly for competitors to imitate

Is this a competency:

- Which competitors will find difficult and costly to imitate, obtain, or substitute for?
- Is this difficulty sustainable because it is not built on unique resources, for example key people can leave or key systems can be acquired?

O – Organisational support, the organisation is appropriately organised to take advantage of the competency

Is this a competency:

*   Which the organisation is well organised to support?
*   For which the organisation has appropriate processes and systems? Sustainable advantage is more often found in competencies around the way resources are managed, developed, and deployed and the way competencies are linked together and integrated.

Combining these answers together as in the following table enables us to clarify which of our competencies are core, that is which can give us **sustained competitive advantage**, and which ones are threshold, that is giving us competitive parity.

Value	Rarity	Inimitability	Organisational Support	Evaluation
Yes or No			No	This creates a **competitive disadvantage**.
Yes	No		Yes	This creates **competitive parity**.
Yes	Yes	No	Yes	This creates a **temporary competitive advantage**.
Yes	Yes	Yes	Yes	This creates a **sustained competitive advantage**.

PERFORMANCE

The purpose of all this analysis has been to find out what the organisation is good at and what it is not good at. It will be important therefore to take a holistic view of this question by looking at overall organisational performance and how it is changing and comparing our performance and competencies to that of our competitors. The former can be addressed by reviewing **accounting measures of performance** and the latter by **benchmarking**. Again, it is essential to recognise the subjective nature of these processes; it is hugely important to conduct a critical assessment of any output.

ACCOUNTING MEASURES OF PERFORMANCE

Accounting ratios – give a basis for comparisons over time and with competitors.
    We should review each of the following as a time series and by comparison with norms in our industry:

*   Gross Profit (sales less costs of sale).
*   Gross Margin (gross profit/sales).

- Profit Margin (profit before tax/sales).
- Return on Capital Employed, ROCE (profit before interest and tax/total assets less current liabilities).

On the basis of these results:

- Is performance improving (or deteriorating)?
- Is performance improving (or deteriorating) at a different rate to that of competitors?

Benchmarking is another means of evaluating our capabilities by understanding how an organisation compares with others – typically competitors. Two approaches can be taken to benchmarking:

- *Industry/sector benchmarking* – comparing performance against other organisations in the same industry/sector using a set of performance indicators, including accounting measures of performance.
- *Best-in-class benchmarking* – comparing an organisation's performance or capabilities against "best-in-class" performance – wherever that is found even in a very different industry.

OVERVIEW OF THE INTERNAL CONTEXT

We can bring all this together by trying to conclude from our analyses on what are our strengths and weaknesses:

- *Strengths* – internal characteristics favourable to our meeting our overall goals.
- *Weaknesses* – internal characteristics that will hinder or limit our reaching our overall goals.

We shall use these conclusions when constructing an overall view of the strategic situation – the **SWOT** (see Chapter 6).

THE MEL CASE

Now and similarly in subsequent chapters, we shall use the MEL case to illustrate the ideas just discussed. You may wish to review the MEL case which was set out in Chapter 1 before proceeding.

Initiating Sarah's project

Sarah's first step was to discuss the situation with the Management Team not only to get their perspective but also to clarify their wishes as the key shareholders in MEL. She knew that in due course it would be necessary to get the input of other stakeholders (employees, key customers, key suppliers), but this would follow her initial analysis of the strategic position.

Conclusion

The Management Team (who have a total shareholding of 25% making them the dominant shareholder if they stuck together) told her that they were all committed to the future success of MEL and all wished personally to be involved. They certainly were not interested, individually or collectively, in selling the business or retiring.

The next step in Sarah's project was to conduct a detailed review of the resources available to MEL.

Box 4.2 How did Sarah do this?

To help her review the MEL resources she met with the Head of HR and the Head of Accounts. As a preliminary step, they produced a list of resources and used it to evaluate them by asking these two questions:

1. **How much of the resource is really available, and is it of suitable quality/condition?** – for example assets on an asset register may be semi-obsolete, staff may be under-motivated and over-worked, factories and equipment may be ill maintained, and so on.
2. **Is it unique/providing a competitive advantage?** – cutting-edge machinery will soon be copied, patents will expire, employee specialist knowledge will become dated – most of what is unique now will be a threshold or, indeed, useless in the future.

Resources audit – outcome

- Physical Resources
  - Factory building on a long commercial lease with 20 years to run. The factory was fully refurbished in 1996 and subsequently well maintained as an engineering workshop.
  - A variety of high-tech machining equipment, mostly purchased in the last 2 years. The head of production regards this machinery as highly flexible and told Sarah that it had a life of 5 to 10 years.
  - Five branded delivery/service vehicles, leased.
  - A range of information technology (IT) equipment providing all the computing power needed by the company, leased.
  - A variety of office and factory furnishings mostly less than 10 years old.

- Human Resources
  - 150 employees, including
    - Administration 8 (average time in employment 2 years, average age 30).
    - Purchasing 3 (average time in employment 2 years, average age 35).
    - Marketing 6 (average time in employment 3 years, average age 38).
    - Design 10 (average time in employment 3 years, average age 35).
    - Production 114 (average time in employment 10 years, average age 50, 30 members over 60).
    - Customer service 4 (average time in employment 4 years, average age 40).
    - Management Team 5 (average time in employment 20 years, average age 61, 2 members over 70).
- Financial Resources
  - Cash at bank £1.7M.
- Intellectual Resources
  - Trademark, the MEL brand.

Conclusion

None of these resources appeared to be unique or in themselves providing a competitive advantage. Three areas of concern were observed:

1. *Human resources offered some causes for concern around a lack of new blood and a lack of sources of new ideas being involved in MEL. This was especially the case in Production and perhaps the Management Team too.*

2. *The factory itself is well maintained but may be rather dated in design and layout compared with more modern workplaces.*

3. *Financial resources still include a substantial amount of cash, but this would be reduced rapidly if current performance is not improved.*

Is it also the case that the company capabilities built on these resources did not really provide any competitive advantage? It might appear this was not the case given the long-term success of MEL. But it seems this might no longer be true; the Management Team had noted that market performance was declining. The worsening customer satisfaction data likely indicate a falling off in previous standards of service quality or that competitors have caught up and perhaps are now offering a better service. The reducing market share, given that the market appears not to be growing, might be due to the new competitors entering the market or a loss of customers due to the worsening service quality; likely, both factors are in play. Neither was it clear to Sarah, at first sight, how well the existing capabilities would be able to respond to the major changes taking place in the automotive industry.

Sarah went on to conduct an analysis of MEL's competencies as one method to address these questions.

Competencies

As head of customer relationship management (CRM), Sarah knew that the customers particularly valued the ability of MEL urgently to deliver specialist components unique to their special requirements. Talking with the Head of Production, she found that this ability was based on several key competencies.

Box 4.3 How did Sarah do this?

Sarah used the VRIO tool to help her understand the competitive value of these competencies:

- Supplier integration.
- Stock management of a wide range of certified specialised materials.
- Design and machining capability always able to take on urgent tasks, often within 24 hours.
- Design and machining capability able to manufacture components to the highest quality with 100% inspection and certification.

She took each of these competencies in turn and evaluated its **Value, Rarity, Inimitability and Organisational Support**:

Value – Does this competence allow us.

- To take advantage of **opportunities** and neutralise **threats?**
- Provide value to customers *but at* a *cost* to us that still allows us to make an acceptable return?

Rarity – Is this competency

- Possessed uniquely by one organisation or only by a few others?
- Is it rare on other than a temporary basis?

Inimitability – Is this a competency

- Which competitors will find difficult and costly to imitate, obtain, or substitute for?
- Is this difficulty sustainable because it is not built on unique resources, for example key people can leave or key systems can be acquired?

Organisational support – Is this a competency

- Which the organisation is well organised to support?
- For which the organisation has appropriate processes and systems?

VRIO analysis outcome

The results of Sarah's VRIO analysis follow.

Supplier integration

Value	Rarity	Inimita-bility	Organisational Support	Evaluation
	Yes or No		No	This creates a **competitive disadvantage**.
Yes		No	Yes	This creates **competitive parity**.
Yes	Yes	No	Yes	This creates a **temporary competitive advantage**.
Yes	Yes	Yes	Yes	This creates a **sustained competitive advantage**.

Stock management

Value	Rarity	Inimita-bility	Organisational Support	Evaluation
	Yes or No		No	This creates a **competitive disadvantage**.
Yes		No	Yes	This creates **competitive parity**.
Yes	Yes	No	Yes	This creates a **temporary competitive advantage**.
Yes	Yes	Yes	Yes	This creates a **sustained competitive advantage**.

Urgent design and machining

Value	Rarity	Inimita-bility	Organisational Support	Evaluation
	Yes or No		No	This creates a **competitive disadvantage**.
Yes		No	Yes	This creates **competitive parity**.
Yes	Yes	No	Yes	This creates a **temporary competitive advantage**.
Yes	Yes	Yes	Yes	This creates a **sustained competitive advantage**.

Quality design and machining

Value	Rarity	Inimita-bility	Organisational Support	Evaluation
	Yes or No		No	This creates a **competitive disadvantage**.
Yes		No	Yes	This creates **competitive parity**.
Yes	Yes	No	Yes	This creates a **temporary competitive advantage**.
Yes	Yes	Yes	Yes	This creates a **sustained competitive advantage**.

Conclusion

There is a temporary competitive advantage in the ability urgently to design and machine bespoke components, but this is likely being reduced by the new competitors, and this is most likely the area in which customer satisfaction is being damaged given that supplier integration, stock management, and quality are threshold, required for successful operations in the sector. Currently then, there is no basis for a sustainable competitive advantage.

Performance

While Sarah was talking with the Head of Accounts, she asked also about financial performance. She was shown the following:

- Profit Margin (Profit before Tax/Sales) has declined from 27% to 17% over the last 3 years.
- Return on Capital Employed, ROCE (profit before interest and tax/total assets less current liabilities) has declined from 67% to 41% over the last 3 years.

Together they concluded that this reflected the marketing data reported to the Management Team, that is:

- Market share declining in the motorsport sector and
- Reputation, as measured by customer satisfaction, being damaged.

Conclusion

Clearly, performance is in rather severe decline!

John and Jerry – a family-owned hairdressing firm

David had some hard thinking to do. Next week he would meet again with the owners of "John and Jerry", a private limited company that ran two hairdressing salons as well as a small, recently opened, café-bar. The owners had asked David to help them tackle some problems that had arisen in their business.

The owners were brothers who had worked in the hairdressing business together since they left school. They had originally both worked for a major hairdressing chain to get the training they needed before setting up on their own 6 years ago. They were both known locally as talented hair stylists. David himself had known them for some years as he ran a successful retail business of his own nearby.

The salons were in the centres of two neighbouring towns and the café-bar was located just down the street from the first salon. The first salon was set up in 2012 in Banbury, the second salon had been opened in 2015 in Witney, and the café-bar had been open for just 1 year. Until fairly recently, they had thought the business was going quite well and had seen no reason why this should change. At their last meeting with David, they had said, "Neither of us is a particularly good planner; we go on our gut instinct, but we haven't done that badly".

But, in the last few months, they had had difficulty in paying themselves the income from the business that they and their families needed. Last week their most important supplier, the hairdressing products company Aveda, had threatened to stop supplying them as the last payment from the business had not been honoured by their bank. Some of the staff had heard of this and were asking to be paid weekly not monthly. Other suppliers had also started to ask for immediate payment.

David asked for some financial information to help him understand the situation. They did not have this immediately but eventually their sister who looked after the finances put together the following data to help David. Their sister was not formally trained but had always liked numbers and enjoyed doing the accounts; she was also responsible for dealing with ordering supplies.

David had visited the two salons and the café-bar and taken the chance to talk to the staff in each location as well as to some of the customers. He had heard that the hairdressing staff felt that their staff restrooms were drab and old-fashioned; along with the rest of both salons, they had last been decorated early in 2013. The staff said they had tried to talk to Adam and Steve about these kinds of issues but did not feel they were listened to. One senior stylist said, "The brothers always decide things for themselves at home and then come and tell us what to do", also

Table 4.1 Trading information provided by the owners

Item - £000	2016		2017		2018		2019			
	Salon 1	Salon 2	Salon 1	Salon 2	Salon 1	Salon 2	Salon 1	Salon 2	Bar - first 6 months	Bar - 2nd 6 months
Net Sales	400	200	500	250	550	310	500	300	70	140
Cost of sales	60	40	100	50	90	70	95	60	30	65
Gross profit	340	160	400	200	460	240	405	240	40	75
Wages	180	120	240	160	300	200	300	200	40	90
Other overheads	44	41	41	42	40	42	38	42	45	10
Bank charges and interest	6	6	7	6	7	6	7	7	2	4
Depreciation	2	2	2	2	3	3	2	2	3	6
Total expenses	232	169	290	210	350	251	347	251	90	110
Net profit	108	-9	110	-10	110	-11	58	-11	-50	-35

NOTE The bar was not set up until 2019

Source: Author's consultancy practice

"You can agree one thing with one of them and then the other says something completely different and the first one then agrees with the other one. You never really know where you stand!" David had noticed from HR records that the turnover of staff from the business had always been quite high.

David also noticed that the shelves on which the Aveda product was displayed seemed rather poorly stocked. David understood from the senior stylist that the direct sale of this product to customers was an important source of income. From asking some of his customers and contacts about the salons, David got the impression that the haircuts themselves were really very good but that the overall service from staff, apart from the owners, was lacklustre. Staff were paid by the hour, and although the rate was quite good, they did not seem very enthusiastic about their jobs. "There's no real training and no future here", he was told and "Just look at the customers – they are not getting any younger and they've all been coming here for years; there's no new people coming in". Susie, the manager of the Witney salon, was particularly unhappy about the owners' way of running the business. "One minute they criticise me for not using my initiative and the next minute they are reorganising my staffing schedules and how I do things without even telling me. It's not clear at all to me what I am supposed to be in charge of, and half the time when I do change anything it gets changed back by one or the other of them". Susie reported that the owners always insist on being told every decision but that she knew very little about what was happening at the Banbury salon, which the owners still directly managed themselves. She thought that their approach might have worked well when they had just the Banbury salon but that it was not so effective now they have grown to 3 separate business locations in two towns.

David's visit to the café-bar (which opened at 11:00 a.m. every day) was during a midweek lunchtime when he expected to find lots of customers who worked in the many shops and offices nearby. In fact, there were only a few people in there; they had dropped in for a coffee as they had been walking past, but there was nobody who seemed to be a regular customer. The menu was inexpensive but was also unexciting, consisting largely of mass-catering options such as pizza. It had lots of choices because the owners felt the more you had available the more you would sell but the result was that it was full of very different types of food with no obvious focus. The manager of the café-bar was Pete; he explained that the main idea was to operate on Friday and Saturday evenings as a bar and nightclub (it stayed open until 2:00 a.m.). The owners had always been interested in music, and they often work as DJ at the bar. They also organised specialist music events with local bands, many of whom they knew well, every month. David noticed that the decoration and style of the café-bar was clearly in tune with this concept, including expensive plasma screens and similar equipment. Interestingly, unlike the hairdressing salons, the café seemed to have very high amounts of stock. Pete said that "they tend to buy in drink and food in huge quantities because then they can get a really good deal. If we are having trouble shifting it we just do a special promotion and slash the price; if you cut the price enough you can usually sell it. Having said that we do end up throwing a lot away".

David had asked the owners to explain how they marketed their business. They were in a hurry to go to a meeting with the "John and Jerry" bank manager but did have time to say that they had no real marketing plan for any of their businesses except for the special music events at the cafe. They had no budget for marketing because they believed that a satisfied customer was the best advertising. David learnt that they were seeing the bank manager to enquire about extending their overdraft or increasing their longer term borrowing as there was no possibility of finding further finance from family resources. They had borrowed money to buy the premises for the café-bar, and their long-term borrowing was now about 45% of their capital employed. "Our long-term plan is to continue growing the business. We'd like to own a number of different businesses, not just hairdressing, and then maybe sell the lot in 20 years and retire. We've got a lot of growing to do before then!" They told him, "We haven't had that many problems in the past. Staff come and go, but we can always replace them. However, we do need to think about what we do next which is why we've called you in. We've heard that one of the big hairdressing chains is opening a salon right next to our Banbury salon and that could be a blow. Do you think you can help us?"

CASE DISCUSSION QUESTIONS

1. Apply the ideas in this chapter to "John and Jerry".
2. What would you conclude were the strengths and weaknesses of the company?

NOTES

1   Barney, J.B. Firm Resources and Sustained Competitive Advantage, *Journal of Management*, vol. 17, no. 1 (1991)

2   Porter, M. *Competitive Advantage: Creating and Sustaining Superior Performance*, New York: The Free Press, 1985

3   Barney, J.B. *Gaining and Sustaining Competitive Advantage*, Reading, MA: Addison-Wesley, 1997

CHAPTER 5

Assessing the strategic context

THE COMPETITIVE ENVIRONMENT

The fundamental and most important question here is clearly to define our industry with clarity and accuracy; else, there is a real danger of overlooking significant strategic issues. Too narrow a definition may overlook important competitors. Too wide a definition runs the risk that the analysis we do will become meaningless. Also, industries often are made up of different markets, for example different geographies or different product or service types which should be analysed separately for similar reasons.

Step 1 – clearly specify the industry within which your project sits. An **industry** is a group of firms producing products and services that are essentially the same and must also be distinguished from a market which is a group of customers for specific products or services that are essentially the same.[1]

Given that students very often get this wrong, it might be helpful to offer some examples (good and bad). It is suggested to use the Abell model.[2] Abell suggests that we define our industry in terms of three dimensions:

1. The served customer groups – who are the customers?
2. The served customer functions – what are the customer's needs?
3. The technologies utilised – how are the needs being satisfied?

For example, suppose that our project revolves around a car repair workshop. We might then define the industry as follows:

1. Individual car owners and managers of company car and light van fleets.
2. The vehicles in question repaired and made roadworthy.
3. Skilled car mechanics and workshop facilities.

However, we might also think, very wrongly, that we should be looking at the whole automotive industry as follows:

1. Individual car owners and managers of company car and light van fleets.
2. To own a car or van for personal or business use.
3. Manufacturing plants located globally, new- and second-vehicle distribution, dealerships, maintenance, fuel supply, valeting services, and so on.

DOI: 10.4324/9781003345398-5

This would be of very little help in thinking clearly about the strategic situation of an individual, or even a chain of car maintenance workshops.

Step 2 – Investigate the **industry structure**; having clearly defined the industry we move on to understand the forces driving competition using **Porter's 5 Forces**[3] model of competition. The following diagram (see Figure 5.1) gives the clearest view of what this is all about. If the forces indicated by arrows are large, then the industry will be very competitive and the opportunity to make good profits will be limited. This is usually referred to as the industry being **unattractive** or, if the forces are small, so that the industry offers the opportunity to make good profits, as it being **attractive**. Our objective in conducting this analysis is to evaluate each of these forces so that we can take a view, overall, as to the attractiveness of the industry. We may then decide to leave the industry or not enter it in the first place. Also, by looking at the details of the operation of each force we can understand how better to position our organisation to take advantage of competitive opportunities and avoid competitive threats.

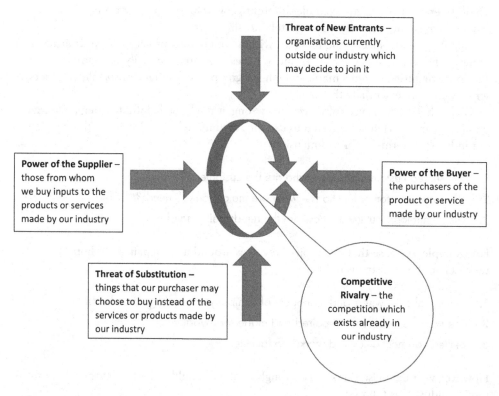

FIGURE 5.1 Porter's 5 Forces view of industry structure

Source: Adapted from Porter, 2008.

The best way to tackle this is to think about each force in turn as follows – be systematic and always look for ways of measuring the forces. Often, these evaluations must be subjective, based on expertise in your industry (your own, a consultant's, or a reputable source).

1. Threat of New Entrants

    If new organisations join the industry, this will increase competitive rivalry, hence driving down the prices that we can charge our customers and tending also to increase the costs of raw materials and other inputs from our suppliers. The result of all this is that profitability is reduced.

    We can evaluate this threat by considering the problems a new organisation might face when seeking to join the industry. For example, do the existing organisations in the industry have an economic advantage because they have grown to a large size? This might be seen in terms of their ability to buy inputs cheaply in bulk or produce more cost-effectively (**economies of scale**) or through their dominance of the industry because of having a large market share (controlling **access to channels** of distribution). Some industries are very expensive to enter, requiring large amounts of start-up capital (e.g. cruise liners). Other industries are protected by limiting legislation (e.g. pharmacy operations). Other factors will occur to you based on experience in the industry. It is important also to consider the risk of effective **competitive retaliation** by the existing organisations in the industry, for example the temporary reduction of prices until the new entrant is driven to failure.

2. Threat of Substitute Products

    The customer's needs that are met by an industry may well also be capable of being met by the different products of another industry. For example, one may take a ferry across the English Channel, or one may take a train. If we have defined our industry as "crossing the English Channel", then these would be competing products covered by Item 5, "Competitive Rivalry". If, however, we have defined our industry as "Ferry Operations" or "Train Operations", then these are substitute products – a ferry journey or a train journey. The decision here is around defining the industry in line with the focus of your analysis.

    The concept of substitution is important because the price to the customer of the substitute, for a given level of performance, sets a limit on the price of the product it substitutes for. If the price we can charge is limited, then the profit we can make is limited.

    There are a couple of important types of substitution and the analyst should always ensure that the risk of both has been considered. They are **product-for-product substitution** (such as the earlier example) and **substitution of need**, where the use of a product or service reduces the customer's need for those of another industry (e.g., purchase of an electric vehicle reduces the need to purchase fossil fuel).

    We can evaluate this threat in terms of our assessment of the degree to which the customer would have to take on additional costs, possibly one-off, to switch to the substitute (known as **switching costs**). This may be in financial terms or operational effort terms, for example changing to a completely new design of operational software, or it may be about overcoming psychological factors such as inertia or brand loyalty.

3. Power of Buyers

    If the buyer is powerful in relation to the organisations making up the industry, then the buyer will have the opportunity to force down the price they pay for a given level of performance. If prices are depressed, then so are profits. An evaluation of this will depend on the various ways a buyer may be powerful and the assessment of the degree of this power relative to the producing industry. Reference is often made to the relative size of the buyers and producers which may, for example, be measured in financial or market share terms. Another approach is to look at the relative number of buyers in the market and the number of producers in the market so that buyers would be powerful if the number of producers was much larger and vice versa. It is worth noticing also that a group of buyers may collectively have the power to affect price even though the individual members of the group could not; for example I don't have power to affect the price of groceries at supermarkets, but if very many of us decided to go to farm shops only, it would certainly impact supermarket prices in due course.

4. Power of Suppliers

If the supplier of the inputs that we use is powerful they can demand higher prices for a given level of performance and thus negatively impact industry profits. Evaluation of this factor is simply the inverse of the points made in relation to the power of the buyer.

5. Competitive Rivalry

When competition amongst the existing organisations in the industry is high this will be reflected in lower profits. We can evaluate this by looking at the structure of the industry, for example are there many similarly sized organisations making up the industry? This will tend to occur if it is easy to enter the industry (low **entry barriers**) or if it is hard to leave the industry (high **exit barriers**). Competition will also be enhanced if the industry is one in which there is low brand loyalty. In analysing the competitive rivalry, we need also to consider the **industry life cycle**. Almost all industries develop over time from a starting point towards an eventual, at least partial, collapse, and the level and type of competitive rivalry vary at points in the life cycle so that identifying the appropriate stage for the industry under analysis will help us evaluate the level of competitive rivalry. To help with this, consider the following diagram (Figure 5.2) and compare it with your knowledge of the operations of the industry under consideration. So, for example, if we are looking at an industry which is mature, then market share can only be acquired at the expense of other members of the industry, creating severe price competition. In this case and in relation to competitive rivalry in general, it is important to consider the cost structure of the industry, if fixed costs are a high proportion of total costs, then organisations will be driven in the direction of high volumes of production and attempt to capture market share by fierce price competition.

Step 3 – We should look now at the competitive geography of our industry. Are there clusters of organisations offering similar products or services for similar prices and produced in the same way? These clusters are called **strategic groups** (Porter 1980) – to give an example: McDonald's and KFC are both in the fast-food strategic group of the restaurant industry. Another group in the same industry offers fine dining; this is a business model which is different from fast food on almost every dimension. Generalising, these two groups offer very different products at very different prices to very different customer segments. It is valuable to know clearly which group we are part of as the other members of the group are our direct competitors. We may also find it valuable to consider the differences between the groups in our industry, perhaps with a view of considering a change

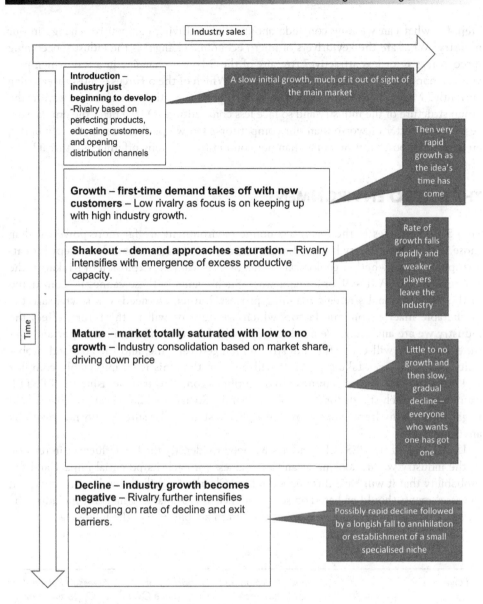

Industry sales

Time

Introduction – industry just beginning to develop -Rivalry based on perfecting products, educating customers, and opening distribution channels

A slow initial growth, much of it out of sight of the main market

Then very rapid growth as the idea's time has come

Growth – first-time demand takes off with new customers – Low rivalry as focus is on keeping up with high industry growth.

Rate of growth falls rapidly and weaker players leave the industry

Shakeout – demand approaches saturation – Rivalry intensifies with emergence of excess productive capacity.

Mature – market totally saturated with low to no growth – Industry consolidation based on market share, driving down price

Little to no growth and then slow, gradual decline – everyone who wants one has got one

Decline – industry growth becomes negative – Rivalry further intensifies depending on rate of decline and exit barriers.

Possibly rapid decline followed by a longish fall to annihilation or establishment of a small specialised niche

FIGURE 5.2 The industry life cycle

of group by adopting a new business model and perhaps to identify if there any unserved customer groups. It is in relation to these thoughts that we should think also about the **critical success factors** we need to have mastered in order to be a success in each strategic group of the industry. These factors are in two parts:

- The fundamental needs of the customers which must be met.
- The ways in which competitive pressures drive successful organisations to act.

Step 4 – what can we now conclude about what is driving competitive change in our industry? What are the key drivers of micro-economic change? Is the industry becoming more attractive or less attractive? Are any of the 5 Forces changing in a way which provides an opportunity or threat for the industry? Which of the 5 Forces is most threatening currently? Might there be an opportunity for our organisation to move to a gap in the group structure of the industry and so face less competition? Do we meet the critical success factors better or worse than our competitors? Do we perform competitively better, creating an opportunity, or worse than our competitors, thereby offering us a threat?

THE MACRO ENVIRONMENT

Step 5 – The forces in the macro-economic environment are far more powerful than those within the industry but tend mostly to act over longer timescales except for catastrophic events, whether geological, social, or political (e.g. explosion of Krakatoa, the emergence of COVID-19, or a major war). Such events as these cannot be considered in the organisational strategic planning process. Rather, we need to ask what are the predictable macro-economic factors which are now, or will in the future, affect the industry we are analysing. We need to know which of these is the most important over time, how they will cause the industry to change over time, and the size and probability of the changes taking place. It will be seen that this is an impossibly complex and immense task and so requires gross simplification. This is done using the PESTEL framework, which stands for Political, Economic, Social, Technological, Ecological and Legal forces. This framework provides a checklist to make sure we do not overlook anything major.

Under each of the PESTEL headings we need to identify the key influences in relation to the industry we are looking at and then assess for each its potential impact and the probability that it will have this impact in fact. Clearly this will always be subjective, but the assessments should be based on such evidence as is available principally including the views of experts in the field. We can set this out in a table such as the following.

Driver	Impact Evaluated on Some Scale, e.g. +5 to –5 (A)	Probability of Occurrence Over an Appropriate Timescale, e.g. 5 years (B)	Assessed Potential as Opportunity or Threat (A) × (B)
Political – say, policies of newly elected government include much greater funding for a key customer type	+4	0.75	+3
Economics – say, inflation in raw material prices expected to worsen	–3	0.5	–1.5

Driver	Impact Evaluated on Some Scale, e.g. +5 to –5 (A)	Probability of Occurrence Over an Appropriate Timescale, e.g. 5 years (B)	Assessed Potential as Opportunity or Threat (A) × (B)
Social – say, ageing population leading to labour shortage	–1	1	–1
Technological – say, recently invented concept that may result in significant reductions in process costs	+2	0.10	+0.2
Ecological – say, exposure of key sources of raw materials to climate change	–3	0.2	–0.6
Legal – say, phased introduction of increases in minimum wage laws	–3	0.8	–2.4

The final column, "Assessed Potential as Opportunity or Threat", indicates the relative assessed size of each of the drivers of change in the macro environment; if shown as positive, they are the source of opportunities, and if shown as negative, they are the source of threats.

Step 6 – Finally, we should combine the outcomes of our micro- and macro-environmental analyses into a single list of significant **Opportunities** and significant **Threats**. We shall then need to seek to develop strategies to take advantage of the former and to avoid the latter. See Chapter 6.

THE MEL CASE

Sarah knew that before she started to think about the external context of MEL, she must clarify her definition of the industry of which MEL is part.

Box 5.1 How did Sarah do this?

She applied the Abell model, which suggests that we define our industry in terms of three dimensions, and in order to get the answers to this clear in her mind, she spoke with members of the Sales Team and Joe Coles, the Director of Production. She asked three questions: who are the customers, what are the customer's needs, and how are the needs being satisfied?

Industry definition outcome

- Customers
  - Car-racing teams.
  - Motorbike-racing teams.
  - British defence manufacturing companies.
  - European defence manufacturing companies.
  - British-owned North Sea operations companies.
  - US-owned North Sea operations companies.
- Customer's needs
  - High-performance components.
  - Full material traceability.
  - Quality plan management.
  - Manufactured from special alloys.
  - Required in a hurry.
  - Bespoke to the individual customer.
- How are the customer's needs being satisfied?
  - Warehousing, stock management, and certification software.
  - Positive Material Identification testing equipment.
  - Best-in-class design software.
  - Enterprise resource planning (ERP) manufacturing software.

Now Sarah moved on to investigate the structure of the industry she had defined.

Box 5.2 How did Sarah do this?

To address these questions, Sarah talked further with Joe Coles and with Jeff Castle and her colleagues in Marketing and the Sales Team. They applied the ideas in Porter's 5 Forces; if these forces are large, then the industry will be very competitive and the opportunity to make good profits will be limited.

The forces are as follow:

- Threat of New Entrants – we can evaluate this threat by considering the problems a new organisation might face on seeking to join the industry.
- Threat of Substitute Products – we can evaluate this threat in terms of our assessment of the degree to which the customer would have to take on additional costs, possibly one-off, to switch to the substitute.
- Power of Buyers – evaluation of this is often made in terms of the relative size of the buyers and producers or the relative number of buyers in the market and the number of producers in the market.
- Power of Suppliers – evaluation of this factor is the inverse of the points made in relation to the power of the buyer.

- Competitive Rivalry —we evaluate this by looking at the structure of the industry; for example are there many similarly sized organisations making up the industry? Is there low brand loyalty? These situations will tend to create severe price competition.

Sarah needed also to consider the industry life cycle. Is the industry mature so that market share can only be acquired at the expense of other members of the industry, or is the industry now in decline which further intensifies rivalry depending on the rate of decline and height of any exit barriers?

The industry Sarah had defined seems to consist just of one group of specialist component providers but those of her colleagues with experience in the broader automotive industry pointed out that component suppliers to the big auto companies could easily compete too if they wished.

Porter's 5 Forces, industry life cycle, and strategic groups outcome

Sarah and her colleagues concluded the following:

- New entrants were beginning to emerge in the industry.
- No substitutes existed, and there was no sign of relevant new technologies.
- Supplier power was high – the industry uses special steels with only a very limited number of specialist suppliers.
- Buyer power was high – the number of motorsport customers has always been limited while the defence and offshore customers were very big organisations and were able easily to switch to other suppliers.
- Competitive rivalry was limited, however – the industry is made up currently of a small group of highly specialised organisations, each with well-established customer relationships.
- A mature industry with signs of decline in the traditional motorsports sector aligned to broader automotive move to electric vehicles (EVs).
- Direct competitors form a strategic group focused on components for the motorsport, defence, and offshore industries.
- The broader automotive components companies are a powerful strategic group with the potential to compete with MEL; some are already making this move.

Conclusion

MEL and its competitors are squeezed between powerful suppliers and powerful buyers tending to push up costs and hold down prices. Also, the emergence of new competitors is tending to increase competitive rivalry. Positive points are that there are no substitute products and competitive rivalry is low, but these by no means outweighed the negatives. Overall then this is rather an unattractive industry in which it will be difficult to be very profitable.

Companies in the broader automotive components industry present a direct threat to MEL and its existing competitors, and this is exacerbated by the mature and to some extent declining nature of the market in relation to traditional motor vehicles.

Critical success factors

The **critical success factors** are the things we need to have mastered in order to be a success in the industry. What these are was Sarah's next question.

Box 5.3 How did Sarah do this?

Critical success factors are built from two parts: first, the fundamental needs of the customers which must be met and, second, the ways in which competitive pressures drive the successful organisation we want to be to act. Sarah's discussions with her colleagues from across MEL all were relevant here. She had asked each of them to give their views on this point.

Critical success factors outcome

The consensus view was as follows:

1. On time response to urgent customer demands
2. Bespoke one-off design
3. Quality performance
4. Certified materials

Conclusion

The Marketing and Sales Teams report that MEL is no longer fully meeting customer expectations. The indications they have are that this revolves particularly around the first critical success factor (CSF).

PESTEL

Having thought her way through understanding the competitive environment around MEL, Sarah knew that she needed now to investigate the macro-environment.

Box 5.4 How did Sarah do this?

We need to ask what are the macro-economic factors which are now, or will in the future, affect the industry we are analysing. We need to know which of these is the most important over time, how they will cause the industry to change over time, and the size, impact, and probability of the changes taking place. This is done using the PESTEL framework to identify the key influences on our industry and assess for each its potential impact and the probability that it will have this impact in fact. We evaluate, subjectively, by

A. impact on some scale, for example +5 to −5 and
B. the probability of occurrence over an appropriate timescale, for example 5 years.

Then we calculate the assessed potential as opportunity (if positive, or +ve) or threat (if negative, or −ve) by calculating A × B

Sarah approached this by reviewing relevant material in quality news sources such *The Times, The Financial Times, The Economist*, BBC News, and others. She then brought together a focus group of her colleagues from across MEL in order to get their input on her ideas.

PESTEL outcome

The consensus which emerged was as follows:

- Politics
  - Global instability leading to increased defence spending (+ve).
  - Pressure better to ensure national energy security (+ve).
- Economics
  - Risk of long-term rises in prices, especially imported special steels, and in interest rates (−ve).
  - Risk of recession or stagflation (−ve).
- Social Change
  - Increasingly negative attitudes to the use of fossil fuels (−ve).
  - Shortages of skills in the workforce (−ve).
- Technological change
  - Rapid developments in EV-related technology.
- Environment
  - COP26 commitments (−ve).
- Law
  - No obvious concerns at present.

Conclusion

There may be increased opportunities among defence market customers. New customer groups are perhaps emerging as the nuclear energy industry is reviving. Also, wind energy is taking centre stage in light of energy security and other fossil fuel–related concerns. Negative attitudes to fossil fuel use will impact traditional motorsport and hasten a move to EV motorsport.

CHAPTER CASE

The organic food industry in Europe

The European organic food market has experienced very strong growth, which is part of a global trend towards healthier eating. Consumers also express growing concerns over animal welfare. The market has been maturing for a few years, and the wide availability of organic products has produced a spectrum ranging from mass-produced budget products to high-priced private labels. This has enabled the market to maintain strong growth despite other signs of maturation. But the performance of the market is now forecast to decelerate. However, market leaders have pointed to a rising awareness of the perceived health benefits of organic food following the pandemic, which could drive further growth in the coming years.

An outline of a Porter's 5 Forces analysis for the European Organic Food industry follows. This analysis includes food retailers in the industry rather than treating them as part of a buying industry:

- *Competitive Rivalry* in the organic foods market is heightened by the lack of product differentiation and negligible switching costs for buyers. However, strong market growth serves to counteract this to some extent.
- *Buyers* have limited power as they are individual consumers. However, consumer demand for organic food drives growth and will likely increase choice as retailers stock a greater variety of organic products.
- *Suppliers* are usually relatively small-scale farmers, whose influence on the market is fairly limited. However, many have integrated forwards and sell directly to end-consumers, strengthening their position to some extent.
- There is a strong threat from non-organic *substitutes*, which are cheaper to buy and are sold in much greater volumes. However, most retailers stock these substitutes alongside, rather than instead of, organic food products.
- *New Entrants* pose a strong threat, since switching costs are relatively low and demand growth is robust.

Source: Marketline, March 2022

CASE DISCUSSION QUESTIONS

1. Restate the 5 Forces analysis if food retailers are instead assumed to be buyers.
2. The preceding analysis is very high level. Take each of the forces and present an analysis of each to substantiate the conclusions given as to its strength.

NOTES

1 Whittington, R., Regnér, P., Angwin, D., Johnson, G. & Scholes, K. *Exploring Strategy*, 12th Edn, Harlow: Pearson, 2021

2 Abell, D.F. *Defining the Business: The Starting Point of Strategic Planning*, Englewood Cliffs: Prentice-Hall, 1980

3 Porter, M. The Five Competitive Forces That Shape Strategy, *Harvard Business Review*, vol. 86, no. 1 (2008)

CHAPTER 6

Assessing and acting on the strategic position

CREATING AND PRESENTING A SWOT ANALYSIS

In this chapter, we bring together the results of our analyses into a single presentation which represents a snapshot of the current strategic position as we have assessed it. It is in the form of a **Strengths, Weaknesses, Opportunities and Threats (SWOT)** analysis. This type of presentation is widely used in management at every level from individual through tactical and operational to strategic. Here we use it in the latter form and the elements which form its parts are defined as follows:

- *Strengths* – internal organisational characteristics favourable to our meeting our goals (see Chapter 4).
- *Weaknesses* – internal organisational characteristics that will hinder or limit our reaching our goals (see Chapter 4).
- *Opportunities* – features in the macro and micro environment that favour us if we can take advantage of them (see Chapter 5).
- *Threats* – features in the macro and micro environment that will cause us to miss our goals if we cannot resist or avoid them (see Chapter 5).

In thinking this through, it is important to be sure that those things we list as opportunities are not things we might do, these would be strategies. They are rather things that may happen or situations that are or may turn to our advantage. At the same time, we must ensure that those things we list as threats are things that may happen outside our own organisation or situations that are or may turn to our disadvantage.

Step 1 – build a SWOT (see Figure 6.1)

First, our analysis of the internal situation will lead to the identification of **Strengths** and **Weaknesses**. The conclusions presented will have emerged from conducting a **resource audit**, the identification of **core competencies**, and from a **review of performance**.

Second, our analysis of the external situation will lead to the identification of **Opportunities** and **Threats** (also known as **key drivers of change**). The conclusions presented will

DOI: 10.4324/9781003345398-6

have come from conducting analyses using **Porter's 5 Forces**, **strategic groups**, **industry life cycle**, **critical success factors**, and **PESTEL**.

The best way to present the SWOT is in the form of a 2 × 2 table as in the imaginary example that follows. To be a practical and useful tool of strategic planning it should include no more than three or, at most, four items in each box. These should be the most important strengths and weaknesses and the most potentially impactful of the opportunities and threats.

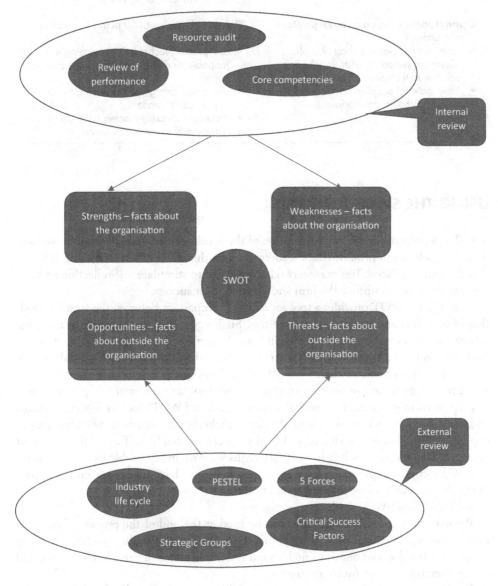

FIGURE 6.1 SWOT and its sources

Strengths shown as bullet points in priority order, e.g.
- Cash in hand in excess of £300M.
- State-of-the-art manufacturing plant.
- Well-established partnerships with agents in all G20 countries.

Weaknesses shown as bullet points in priority order, e.g.
- Current products are near the end of their life cycles.
- New-product development pipeline ineffective.
- Serious skilled labour shortages in areas of all manufacturing plants.

Opportunities shown as bullet points in priority order, e.g.
- Both key competitors short of cash.
- Customer switching costs very high in relation to their size.
- Raw material supplier base consists of many small organisations.

Threats shown as bullet points in priority order, e.g.
- 3D printing technology increasingly capable of delivering a substitute product type.
- Spiralling energy prices driving major input cost increase.
- Political instability worsening in areas where raw material is sourced.

USING THE SWOT ANALYSIS

SWOT is a powerful mode of presentation of the results of the strategic analysis we have done. By itself, it will prompt senior leaders to much thought and soul-searching. It forces that the truth be faced. Top managers rely on SWOT to stimulate self-reflection and discussions on how to improve the firm and position it for success.

In addition, SWOT provides a tool for a direct comparison between the strategic position of ourselves and of our key competitors. Such key competitors will be in the same strategic group as we are, and so they will have the same opportunities and threats as we do. If we can form a realistic view of their strengths and weaknesses, then we shall be able to estimate the content of their own SWOT analyses (a tip here, if you want to know about the strengths and weaknesses of your competitors, then ask your salespeople – they face up to them every day). Now that we have a set of SWOTs for our key competitors and ourselves, we can compare them. We can ask whether our strengths will enable us to exploit their weaknesses or vice versa. Equally, we can use our SWOT as a direct source of strategic ideas asking ourselves how the strengths we have might enable us to take advantage of the opportunities and whether the weaknesses we have might worsen the impact of the threats and how we might respond to this.

Step 2 – Using SWOT to develop a strategy

We have seen that SWOT analysis can be used at the end of the process of environmental and organisational analysis to synthesise strategic review findings and diagnose key issues. In doing this, our aim is to understand the implications of the overall internal and external analysis for our future strategy.

The best approach to this is to take our SWOT analysis one step further by setting up a tabulation of pair comparisons of all the possible combinations of each of the S, W, O and T. We can then identify strategies (action plans) which can turn each of these pair comparisons to the best possible advantage:

- We shall be seeking to use strengths to take advantage of opportunities and to defend against threats thus leading to enhanced competitive advantage overall.
- Also we shall be seeking to identify how weaknesses might negate opportunities and create exposure to threats so that the weaknesses can be addressed in the most effective way overall and make our competitive advantage more sustainable.

The following table gives an imaginary example, building on the SWOT set out earlier, of how we can use the analyses we have done directly to generate strategic ideas. But it must be noted that this is not in itself a sufficient approach to strategy generation as will be seen in the next chapter.

	Strengths S1 Cash in hand in excess of £300M S2 State-of-the-art manufacturing plant S3 Well-established partnerships with agents in all G20 countries	**Weaknesses** W1 Current products are near the end of their life cycles W2 New-product development pipeline ineffective W3 Serious skilled labour shortages in areas of all manufacturing plants
Opportunities O1 Both key competitors short of cash O2 Customer switching costs very high in relation to their size O3 Raw material supplier base consists of many small organisations	S1O1 – Buy competitors? S1O3 – Buy suppliers? S3O1 – Further development of international activities?	W1O2 – Enhance switching costs (e.g. offer a more bespoke product) to lengthen product life
Threats. T1 3D printing technology increasingly capable of delivering a substitute product type T2 Spiralling energy prices driving major input cost increase T3 Political instability worsening in areas where raw material is sourced	S1T1 – Buy a company developing the technology? S1T3 – Develop new sources of supply?	Nothing obvious here – a worrying situation!

Keep up to date

Additionally, even so far as SWOT goes, it is not adequate to create a SWOT and then move on. The SWOT must continuously be kept up to date. This requires that the analysis we have conducted in the previous chapters is converted into a process of continuous scanning of the internal and external environments of our organisation.

We must set up a continuous process of conducting audits of both our resources and our micro- and macro-environments – keeping our eyes open, not resting on our laurels!

There are three important dangers of which to be aware:

- SWOT, simply because it is such a powerful presentation can become the end. But not only will it rapidly become out of date, but also the apparent strengths we have identified may not lead to an advantage, for example if they turn out not to be appropriate to the needs of the market or the mission or strategy of the firm.
- Second, the focus of SWOT on the external environment tends often to be too narrow, missing the need or opportunity to redefine an industry boundary and thereby take a broader view.
- Third, SWOT can overemphasise a single element of strategy without identifying its downside; for example excessive reliance on a strength in low-cost production may result in poor press, a damaged reputation, and labour relations problems.

THE MEL CASE

Sarah was now in a position to pull together an overview of the current strategic position of MEL into a SWOT.

Box 6.1 How did Sarah do this?

Working from all of the material she had collected together Sarah asked herself what Strengths, Weaknesses, Opportunities, and Threats she had identified:

- **Strengths** – internal organisational characteristics favourable to our meeting our goals (see Chapter 4).
- **Weaknesses** – internal organisational characteristics that will hinder or limit our reaching our goals (see Chapter 4).
- **Opportunities** –features in the macro and micro-environment that favour us if we can take advantage of them (see Chapter 5).
- **Threats** – features in the macro- and micro-environment that will cause us to miss our goals if we cannot resist or avoid them (see Chapter 5).

- SWOT outcome
  - Strengths
    - Best-in-class design capability with suppliers closely integrated, allowing co-creation of products to meet bespoke demands.
    - Significant cash reserves.
  - Weaknesses
    - Manufacturing wastage rates higher than industry norms.
    - Age distribution of employees in key areas likely to result in substantial loss of skills and company knowledge.
  - Opportunities
    - Impact of energy shortages and climate change creating opportunities in the renewables sector (wind and nuclear).
    - Growth of electric vehicle motorsport sector by type and by new entrants.
  - Threats
    - New entrants in the motorsport components market.
    - Long-term decline of traditional motorsport as the automotive sector moves to wholly electrical.

This SWOT was then used by Sarah as the basis for thinking through possible strategies.

Box 6.2 How did Sarah do this?

Sarah set up a tabulation of pair comparisons of all the possible combinations of each of the S, W, O, and T. She then again assembled her focus group of colleagues and with their help identified strategies (action plans) which could turn each of these pair comparisons to the best possible advantage:

- Seeking to use strengths to take advantage of opportunities and defend against threats, thus leading to enhanced competitive advantage overall.
- Seeking to identify how weaknesses might negate opportunities and create exposure to threats so that the weaknesses can be addressed in the most effective way overall and make our competitive advantage more sustainable.

Conclusion in the form of a TOWS analysis

	Strength 1	Strength 2	Weakness 1	Weakness 2
Opportunity 1	Design products to meet needs of wind energy and nuclear sectors	Identify opportunities to invest in specialist suppliers already operating in the wind/nuclear energy sectors	Improve processes/ skills to mitigate the risk that product delivered to wind energy and nuclear sectors will be high-priced or poor quality	Establish remedial recruitment and knowledge management processes to fill gaps before they appear
Opportunity 2	Design products and re-orient supplier base to meet the needs of new electric motorsport types	Identify opportunities to invest in specialist suppliers capable of meeting the needs of new electric motorsport types	Improve processes/ skills to mitigate the risk that product delivered to emerging electric motorsport will be high-priced or poor quality	Establish remedial recruitment and knowledge management processes to fill gaps before they appear
Threat 1	Develop design and supply capability to include electric vehicle (EV) specialities reducing non-EV committed capability	Identify opportunities to invest in specialist suppliers capable of meeting the needs of new electric motorsport types	Improve processes/ skills to mitigate the risk that product delivered to the motorsport sector will be high-priced or poorer quality than that of the new competitors	Establish remedial recruitment and knowledge management processes to fill gaps before they appear
Threat 2	Re-orient design and supply capability to non-traditional automotive markets.	Identify opportunities to invest in specialist suppliers capable of meeting the needs of new electric motorsport types	Accelerate exit from the declining traditional motorsport market	Establish remedial recruitment and knowledge management processes to manage the decline in traditional automotive activity while retaining knowledge and key skills relevant to future markets

CHAPTER CASE

Bayer AG

Bayer AG is a life sciences company. The company offers prescription and non-prescription medical products, cosmetics, seeds, plant traits, chemical, and biological crop protection products. It also offers products and solutions for the prevention and treatment of diseases in animals. The company markets its products under the Adalat, Redoxon, Baytril, Xofigo, Nativo, Serenade, Canesten, Afrin, Cydectin, and Seresto brand names. Bayer distributes its products directly to farmers and through pharmacies, retailers, wholesalers, hospitals, veterinarians, supermarkets, and drugstore chains. It has a business presence throughout the world and is headquartered in Leverkusen, Germany.

Strengths

- Robust focus on research and development to develop innovative products.
- Strong distribution network and wide geographical presence reduces business risk.

Weaknesses

- Low liquidity that could limit growth opportunities.

Opportunities

- Increase in food prices.
- Positive outlook for global pharmaceutical industry.

Threats

- Price control over drugs.
- Risks associated with manufacturing operations.
- Intense competition.

Source: Marketline Sept 2022

CASE DISCUSSION QUESTIONS

1. Use the Bayer global website (www.bayer.com/) and an investigation of the websites of its key competitors (GlaxoSmithKline Plc, Eli Lilly and Company, Johnson & Johnson, Novartis AG, Merck & Co Inc, and Pfizer Inc) to seek to substantiate the SWOT set out earlier. Add detail to the points mentioned so that their impact can be evaluated.

2. Now construct a TOWS analysis. What possible strategies would you suggest to the senior management of Bayer.

CHAPTER 7

Identifying strategic options

CONTENTS OF THIS CHAPTER

In the last chapter, we saw how the use of SWOT brought all of our strategic analysis together in one place and how it could be used directly to inspire some strategic ideas. But these will necessarily be ideas inspired by what we have found out, they will tend to be reactive rather than proactive and will be limited therefore in scope and perhaps be lacking in innovation. In this chapter, we take a different approach. We ask what types of strategies exist in principle and whether any of those strategies could be relevant to a better delivery of the organisational mission.

First, we can focus on the business we are currently in, that is ask the question, "How can we operate more effectively providing our existing product or service to our existing customers?" If our organisation operates in multiple businesses, then we can ask this question of each business separately, but we shall also want to consider corporate strategies as discussed later. In both cases, we shall wish also to consider the various methods available to us to deliver our strategic concepts.

GENERIC BUSINESS STRATEGIES

There are two related ways of looking into the business strategies that may help us to operate more effectively in our existing business. These are **Porter's Generic Business Strategies**[1] and the **strategy clock**.[2] They both provide a framework to guide our thinking. The former looks at the different ways in which we might generate competitive advantage and the latter looks at the different offers we might make to our customers in terms of their perception of value for money.

To apply Porter's ideas, we need to look at the pros and cons, for us, of each of the four generic strategies set out in Figure 7.1.

Cost leadership strategy

This involves having sustainably lower costs than the industry average while maintaining at least average quality. The advantage of this is that we can sell at industry average prices but get greater than average profits from each sale. If it can be achieved this is the most effective business strategy, but how to do it?

DOI: 10.4324/9781003345398-7

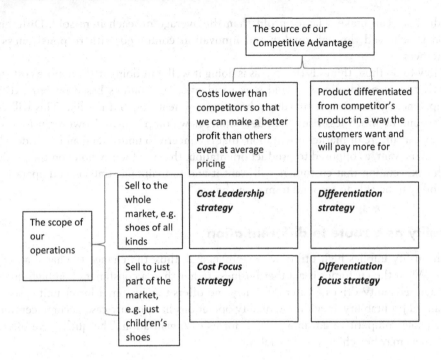

FIGURE 7.1 Generic strategies

Source: Adapted from Porter, 1985.

Costs can be kept low compared to the average in several ways:

- Buy inputs more cheaply than the average but of the required specification and quality through bulk purchasing or buyer power in the market (**economies of scale**).
- Use inputs more efficiently by reducing waste through **improved operations** or delivering more outputs through improved processes or improved **labour productivity** or improved use of **working capital.**

In a mature industry, this strategy is likely to be highly lucrative. However, if the industry is young or inherently or currently dynamic (e.g. a time of technological innovation) it will be difficult to maintain these relative advantages in the long term, and of course, many of them are more or less easily imitable.

Differentiation strategy

A firm differentiates its products from those of its competitors in a way that makes them appeal more to customers, across the whole market. Customers must also be willing to pay for this difference. Thus, we can charge above-average prices and providing the extra we can charge is significantly more than the extra costs of our differentiated product we can make a larger profit than the average on each item sold. Differentiation is achieved through **quality** and **innovation** combined with **responsiveness to customers**.

How to do these things is the key, as is doing it well, but doing it at no more cost than strictly necessary. Ideally, we could seek to identify possibilities based on our existing competencies, for example by adding benefits, new features, and the like. This will cost far less and be much less risky than developing new competences. However, it is crucial to adopt a culture of **market orientation**, that is concern to understand and provide what customers want, as opposed to **product orientation**, that is a focus wholly on the product in the expectation that customers will want it and to maintain strategic and operational flexibility to be able to respond to market change.

Quality as a route to differentiation

High quality implies high utility to customers and, thus, the chance to charge a higher price. When the customer is another business rather than a consumer, then high quality, through reliability, drives greater efficiency and offers the customer lower unit costs and enhanced profitability. In addition, quality operations have in any case become central to sustainable competitive advantage in all forms of organisation. The quality we offer to customers may be achieved in several ways:

- **Excellence** – for example design, features and functions, level of service attached, and the like.
- **Reliability** – for example does what it is designed to do, does it well, rarely breaks down, and so on.
- **Fitness for purpose** – does exactly the things needed and no more, bespoke perhaps.

Innovation as a route to differentiation

Product innovation means creating a new product or a new version of an existing one with superior attributes thus creating more customer utility. By contrast, **process innovation** is the creation of new ways of making or delivering products. This may also create more customer utility (e.g. shopping online). But generally, it allows for reduced production costs. If we are able to do both of these things, then substantial benefits will accrue.

Responsiveness as a route to differentiation

Superior responsiveness to customers implies the ability better to identify customer's needs. It is driven by a deep understanding of the market and customer needs. This will create extra customer utility compared to that offered by competitors through the application of superior quality and innovation capability.

Focus

Focus is about selecting a narrow range of customers from the broader market and focusing closely on their specific needs.

Differentiation focus

Differentiation focus is therefore about taking the ideas under the earlier heading of differentiation strategy and applying them to this selected segment of the market. This may well offer a way in which we can achieve differentiation using our existing competencies or a way in which we can build new competencies at a limited extra cost. The fact that there can be only a relatively small number of customers, of course, means that a price premium is even more necessary.

Cost focus

Cost focus deals with the case of a market segment for which a premium price is unlikely to be achieved. If this is the case costs need to be driven down somehow even though **economies of scale** will not be available. For example, this could be suitable for a local firm with low costs overall because of physical closeness to customers.

The strategy clock

The strategy clock (see Figure 7.2) offers an alternative approach which is more focused on the customer, looking at the price they will have to pay and their perception of the added value they will achieve from the purchase, both being compared with the offer of competitors.

No-frills strategy

The focus in this case is solely on price-sensitive segments of the market. The product or service offered is reduced to the most basic version, providing for the minimal needs of the customer. This may be attractive as a means of market entry, gaining operational and market experience through winning market share. This experience could then be used as a basis for expansion and strategy development.

Low-price strategy

This strategy seeks to offer a lower price than competitors while trying to maintain similar perceived added value. Unit margins will be low and if the industry is highly competitive these margins will be reduced even further. Low margins imply an inability to reinvest significantly. It can be a successful approach if the organisation can achieve lower prices

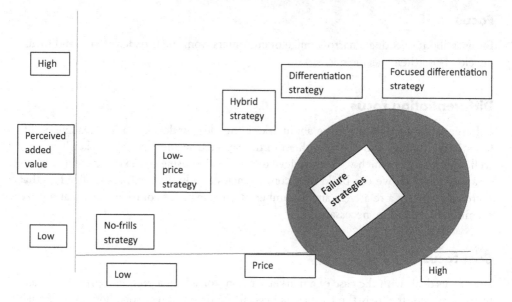

FIGURE 7.2 The strategy clock

Source: Adapted from D. Faulkner & C. Bowman, *The Essence of Competitive Strategy*, Prentice Hall, 1995.

via sustainable lower costs but can nevertheless offer the same or similar added value compared to the competition. Potentially this could be achieved via a significant existing market share from an earlier no-frills operation or perhaps via substantial external investment.

Hybrid strategy

Here we seek simultaneously to achieve differentiation and a price lower than that of competitors. Good as well as cheap is always a very attractive combination so this would assist in building market share, which in turn would generate further cost advantages. In this way, it can be an effective entry strategy, but the combination of competences required to enable "good and cheap" is often difficult to create.

Differentiation strategy

As in Porter's **Generic Strategies**, this approach seeks to provide products/services different from competitors in ways valued by buyers while charging somewhat higher prices. See the earlier discussion of this strategy.

Focused differentiation

As in Porter's **Generic Strategies**, this approach seeks to provide high perceived value, justifying a substantial price premium. See the earlier discussion of this strategy.

Failure strategies

These fall into three categories to be avoided:

- High price/Standard value – extremely high risk of losing market share.
- High price/Low value – only feasible in a monopoly situation protected by entry barriers.
- Standard price/Low value – very high risk of losing market share.

CORPORATE STRATEGIES

Corporate strategy focuses on asking the question, "What businesses, often called **strategic business units** or **SBUs**, should we invest in so as to achieve our goals?"

First, we might look at the direction in which to develop each of our existing businesses beyond present limits using **Ansoff's Matrix**[3] (see Figure 7.3). This is sometimes referred to as the question of **strategic direction**.

Consolidation strategy

This involves protecting and strengthening the current position. If a larger market share results, then there will be improvements in the following:

- Economies of scale.
- Brand strength.

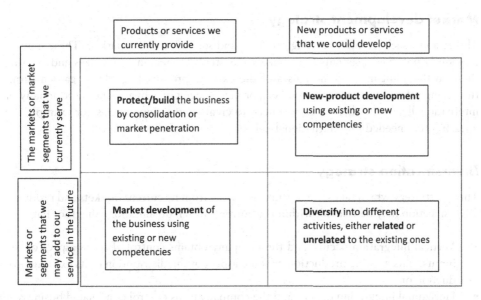

FIGURE 7.3 Ansoff's Matrix

Source: Adapted from H.I. Ansoff, 1988.

- Ability to compete on quality.
- Position during the maturity phase of the life cycle.

Implementing this strategy is likely to require reshaping the organisation, innovation in processes, and downsizing activities that are less profitable.

Market penetration strategy

A strategy which will result in gaining market share; achieving this will depend on the following:

- Nature of the market, if it is growing, mature or shrinking.
- Availability of significant additional resources.
- Complacency of market leaders such that they will allow this to happen.

New-product development strategy

The development and delivery of significantly modified or new products or services to existing markets. This can occur in two ways: it may be possible to use existing competencies, typically identifying and following developing customer requirements or with the development of new competencies typically when the existing **critical success factors** (CSFs) no longer offer a competitive advantage, and the **CSFs** are changing. Clearly, the former offers lower risk, lower cost opportunities whereas in the latter case, it is quite likely that new competitors possessing the new **CSFs** are already achieving success in the market.

Market development strategy

This strategy seeks to offer existing products and services to new markets. These may be previously unserved segments (e.g. making children's trainers in larger sizes and offering them to the adult market), new uses of the existing product (e.g. plastic garden furniture being offered to the events market), or new geographies by expanding regionally or internationally. Again, there may be a need to create new competencies, for example the infrastructure needed for international delivery.

Diversification strategy

This is a strategy which takes the organisation away from its current markets and products. Diversification may be **related**, within the current overall organisational field so that:

- **Vertical integration** occurs, and the company obtains control of some aspect of the inputs to its existing production or some aspect of the distribution of its existing production or.
- **Horizontal integration** occurs, and the company gains control of a related business at the same level as its own position in the supply chain; for example an online clothing retailer purchases an online household goods retailer.

Benefits of the former are likely to be around retaining more of the overall profit in the supply chain in the hands of the diversifying organisation. Benefits of the latter are likely to be around sharing resources and competencies, thus enhancing overall profitability.

Or diversification may be **unrelated**. The benefit of moving into a completely unrelated field is likely to be wholly financial; it is really an investment strategy delivering corporate growth. Diversification needs caution. It is by far the riskiest of all the Ansoff strategies, and experience shows that excessive diversification, especially if unrelated, dilutes the management's resources to the point at which significant disbenefit occurs.

Portfolio analysis

Second, we might wish to look at the set of businesses that we operate and ask whether, taken together, they are a coherent, effective, and sustainable **portfolio** of investments which are well directed towards our goal. There are a number of approaches, but the most commonly used framework is the Boston Consulting Group or **BCG Matrix** also known as the Growth/Share matrix[4] described here (see Figure 7.4).

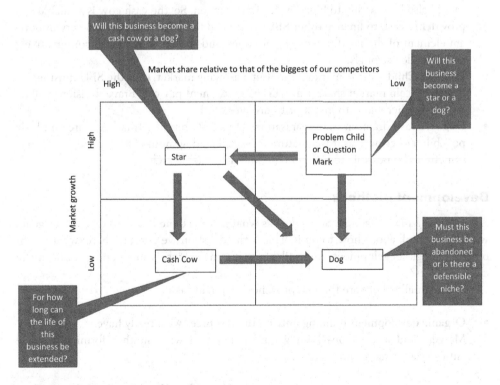

FIGURE 7.4 The Boston Consulting Group Matrix

Source: Adapted from P. Regner, G. Johnson, & K. Scholes, *Exploring Strategy*, 12th Edn, Pearson, 2021.

The vertical axis of the matrix is the rate of market growth (so that high growth implies high cash consumption as we invest to meet demand). The horizontal axis is relative market share, that is the market share of the organisation being studied compared with that of its largest competitor (so that a high value implies market dominance, good profitability, and hence high cash production). The arrows show the route that a typical strategic business unit will take over its life cycle. A particular point here is that a **problem child** may or may not become a **star** and that a **star** may or may not become a **cash cow**.

We can use this idea to look at our set of SBUs as a whole, that is as a portfolio of investments. We can ask if it is a balanced portfolio so that the cash generation of our cash cows is sufficient to support the investment needs of our stars and problem children. It draws our attention to the actions needed in relation to each of the SBUs and will thereby colour the strategic decisions made at the business level:

- **Star** – This SBU will need to spend heavily to gain market share; in a growing market, all competitors are trying to get customers and will have to spend heavily. It is particularly important to invest in improvements that will ensure that a star becomes a cash cow rather than a dog as the rate of market growth slackens. This depends on maintaining market dominance against new entrants.
- **Cash Cow** – This SBU has a high market share in a mature market. Thus, stability exists and less expenditure is needed on marketing and other investments. Unit costs should also be low due to high levels of production. So, the cash cow is available as a provider of cash to finance other SBUs that need this. The cash cow is a very important element of the portfolio, its engine room, and should be managed conservatively and defended strongly.
- **Problem Child** – Little market share but a growing market, thus the SBU must invest heavily to gain market share. But will the investment pay off? Brave decisions will be required either way – to invest or to disinvest?
- **Dog** – A cash drain on the organisation – this SBU has little market share and little possibility of growth as it is a mature market. The dog should be dropped, but it may sometimes be possible to differentiate into a profitable niche.

Development methods

A strategy is a plan of action. So, as well as what is to be done better to deliver our goals, we have to think about how to do it. This is the question we consider here: what methods of strategic development are available to us and which is most appropriate in the circumstances?

Fundamentally, there are three approaches we might take:

- **Organic development** building only on the resources we already have.
- **Mergers and acquisitions** joining our organisation with another forming a single entity by agreement or purchase.

- **Joint developments and alliances of various sorts** agreeing with other organisations to work together towards some joint end while remaining separate entities.

Organic development

There is no steady state in a competitive market, an organisation is either growing and developing in some way or it is declining and will eventually fail. Accordingly, all organisations must be developing continuously in all sorts of short and medium term, big and small ways. All of this is internal development, and when this ethos is applied to strategic change, typically longer term and larger in impact, the term applied is **organic development**.

There are a range of motives which might drive this organic development:

- To develop new competitive competencies, for example if we are developing new products or services, doing this ourselves means that we should more easily understand how best to sell them.
- To spread out the cost, starting small and taking time, if we do not have the resources for the major up-front investment required by an acquisition.
- If there is no suitable partner or acquisition available, perhaps we may be developing a completely new type of venture so no other player exists.
- To avoid cultural problems arising internally or with a new partner or acquisition, often a cause of the failure of mergers and acquisitions.

Mergers and acquisitions

Mergers and acquisitions offer many benefits if the resources and a suitable target exist:

- Speedy to implement, this may be a crucial consideration in very dynamic situations.
- Reducing competitive reaction, if this is a new market for us, then it avoids our being a new entrant, and it avoids creating excess capacity serving the market.
- This is a way to gain or protect market share by reducing the number of competitors.
- There may be financial opportunities such as the target being undervalued.
- It enables the acquisition of resources and competencies, for example research and development expertise, knowledge of a market, and so on.
- There may be ways to generate cost-efficiency by reducing duplication and rationalising provision.
- Key stakeholders, particularly institutional shareholders, may have expectations of growth and enhanced market value, quickly generated in this way.

But mergers and acquisitions do not always produce the promised benefits. This is typically due to:

- Paying too much for the acquisition in a competitive auction,
- Unexpected problems are discovered because of poor **due diligence**, and
- The synergies hoped for do not emerge; this is often because problems of cultural fit emerge so that the new organisation becomes less effective and efficient than either of the predecessor organisations separately.

Alliances

Alliances are increasingly important and may often offer a better way forward than either of the preceding approaches. This is especially so in the following circumstances:

- There is a need for critical mass to provide for economical operations, joining with competitors or providers of **complementary products** could provide this much more easily than growing in other ways.
- The potential partner or partners are specialists and can provide activities that best match their individual resources and competencies.
- The potential partner has expert knowledge in the market, for example making a first e-commerce entry with a partner which already has this experience.

There are many forms of alliance each appropriate for different circumstances:

- **Joint ventures** are alliances in which the partners remain independent but set up a newly created organisation jointly owned by the parents.
- **Consortia** are alliances in which several partners agree to a **joint venture** designed to undertake a particular project and usually having a formal arrangement specifying profit and control split.
- **Networks** are informal collaborations based on mutual advantage and trust, for example in the airline industry where passengers can use several 'partner' airlines whilst travelling on a single ticket.
- **Opportunistic alliances** are informal arrangements around a particular project.
- **Franchising** is a collaboration in which each **franchisee** undertakes specific activities, for example manufacture, distribution, and selling, and the **franchiser** is responsible for other activities that are held centrally, for example brand management, marketing, and training.
- **Licensing** gives the licensee the right to produce all aspects of a product or service and is granted for a fee.
- **Subcontracting** occurs when a company is contracted to provide a specific service, for example catering and cleaning.

Factors influencing the choice of alliance type are set out in the following table.

	Form of Relationship		
	Loose	Contractual	Ownership
	• Networks	• Licensing	• Consortia
	• Opportunistic alliances	• Franchising	• Joint ventures
		• Subcontracting	
Influencing factors			
A The Market			
• Speed of market change	Fast change		Slow change
B Resources			
• Asset management	By each partner separately		Managed together
• Partner's assets	Draw on partner's assets		Dedicated to alliance
• Risk of losing resource to partner	High risk		Low risk
C Expectations			
• Financial risk	Maintains risk		Dilutes risk
• Political climate	Unfavourable climate		Favourable climate

To be successful, there are some key ingredients of alliances:

- There needs to be trust in the partner's competence and intentions.
- Senior management support: alliances require inter-organisational working relationships to be formed and senior management in both organisations can smooth the political and cultural problems.
- Compatibility between the organisations is also essential to building strong working relationships at all levels.
- Clear, agreed-on goals and objectives are set out and jointly monitored.
- Performance expectations must be defined clearly and must be seen to be met requiring a willingness to share information.
- Flexibility will allow the alliance to evolve and change just as any other entity must.

INTERNATIONAL STRATEGY

It will be evident that all the development methods mentioned earlier could be undertaken in the home market or could be combined with an international strategy opening up new markets in different parts of the world. When the approach adopted includes the acquisition of a substantial stake in a foreign business or buying it outright or expanding operations directly to a new region by creating a new operation from scratch, it is called **foreign direct investment**.

The key choices which are specific to the international nature of the strategy and are added to those addressed earlier in the "Development Methods" subsection are how to respond to globalised competition and how to respond to the local demands of the new market:

- It may be that the industry is one in which there is a need for **global efficiency**; that is the cost pressures of operating internationally in the relevant industry override those operating locally, or it may be that this is not the case. For example the former would be the case if low labour cost production and global distribution were the norm whereas the latter would be the case when that low labour cost production was actually in the home country.
- Second, it may be that the industry is one in which there is a requirement in the industry to offer products or services that are, or appear to be, locally sourced and or targeted; that is there is a need for **local responsiveness**, or this may not be the case. For example a product or service that meets the needs of very specific local cultures and tastes such as national cuisines or one which is fundamentally the same worldwide such as road vehicles.

Combining these characteristics will give rise to four possible strategies:[5]

- **International Strategy** – the firm uses the core competency or firm-specific advantage it developed at home as its main competitive weapon in the foreign market it enters. But there will be a lack of local responsiveness and the inability to realise any available location economies. Failure to exploit **experience curve** effects as no new experience will be developed beyond those existing already at home.
- **Global Strategy** – the firm views the world as a single marketplace, and its primary goal is to create standardised goods and services that will address the needs of customers worldwide. It offers the ability to exploit global experience-curve effects and global economies, but at the same time, there is a lack of local responsiveness.
- **Multi-Domestic Strategy** – the firm views itself as a collection of relatively independent operating subsidiaries, each of which focuses on a specific domestic market. But there will be an inability to realise any economies beyond those available in each locality and a failure to exploit any experience-curve effects beyond those developed locally. Also, there will be a failure to transfer distinctive competencies to overseas markets even if they would have value.
- **Transnational Strategy** – the firm attempts to combine the benefits of global-scale efficiencies with the benefits of local responsiveness. The ability to exploit global experience-curve effects and global economies also offers the ability to customise

products to location. But the difficulties in implementation due to the highly complex organisational problems arising must not be underestimated.

We need to identify how these characteristics apply in our organisational context so that an assessment can be made of which approach seems most appropriate.

THE MEL CASE

From the TOWS Sarah has a wide set of practical ideas about what might be done, but she also wants to know what possible types of strategy may be relevant for her to look into.

Box 7.1 How does Sarah do this?

There are two related ways of looking into the business strategies that may help MEL to operate its existing business more effectively. These are **Porter's Generic Business Strategies** and the **strategy clock**. Both provide frameworks to guide our thinking. The former looks at the different ways in which we might generate competitive advantage, and the latter looks at the different offers we might make to our customers in terms of their perception of value for money.

Porter offers four possible strategies derived from the study of the market being addressed (a special part of the market or the whole market) and the source of competitive advantage (seeking to offer something special that customers will pay more for or seeking to minimise our operating costs):

- Cost Leadership.
- Differentiation.
- Cost Focus.
- Differentiation Focus.

The strategy clock offers an alternative approach which is more focused on the customer, looking at the price they will have to pay and their perception of the added value they will achieve from the purchase, both compared with the offer of competitors. The clock suggests that there are five broad types of strategy:

- No Frills.
- Low Price.
- Hybrid.
- Differentiation.
- Focused Differentiation.

Sarah referred to her notes from discussions with Marketing, Sales, and Operations colleagues, asking herself how she would describe the MEL market and offer to customers using the frameworks of Porter and the strategy clock.

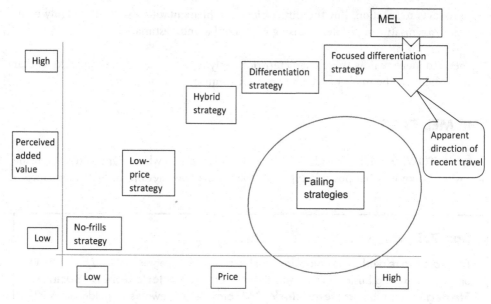

FIGURE 7.5 Application of the strategy clock to MEL

Source: Adapted from Faulkner and Bowman, *The Essence of Competitive Strategy*, Prentice Hall, 1995.

Generic strategies and the strategy clock outcome

MEL seems certainly to be following a differentiation focus strategy at present. It is focused on a very narrow part of the automotive market and a couple of other specialist markets for its products. The challenge seems to be whether it is differentiating successfully.

The strategy clock, with its emphasis on customer perception of the added value they will achieve from the purchase, indicated a worrying direction of travel for MEL (see Figure 7.5) as its position on the clock approaches the "failing strategies".

Conclusion

A firm differentiates its products from those of its competitors in a way that makes them appeal more to customers across the whole market, and yet it seems from the data presented by Jeff Castle that customers are increasingly dissatisfied. Differentiation is achieved through quality and innovation combined with responsiveness to customers – these seem then to be areas in which MEL needs to make improvements.

A solution could be to reduce prices so as to align with perceived added value, but this seems unlikely to be effective as the customers served by MEL are not especially price-sensitive and are much more concerned about quality and delivery on demand. Perhaps MEL might seek to serve a broader range of customers across the general automotive and fixings market. But this would mean entry into an already-mature and highly competitive part of the market.

Ansoff's Matrix

Sarah wanted also to consider whether MEL should perhaps be looking at new products or perhaps at completely new markets for their products.

Box 7.2 How does Sarah do this?

She might look at the direction in which to develop our existing business beyond present limits using Ansoff's Matrix, which offers four strategies.

Consolidation and Market Penetration Strategy – this involves protecting and strengthening the current position if consolidating and taking customers away from other suppliers if seeking to penetrate the market more deeply.

New-Product Development Strategy – this involves the development and delivery of significantly modified or new products or services to existing markets. This can occur in two ways: it may be possible to use existing competencies, typically identifying and following developing customer requirements, or by developing new competencies, typically when the existing critical success factors no longer offer a competitive advantage.

Market Development Strategy – this strategy seeks to offer existing products and services to new markets. These may be previously unserved segments or new uses of the existing product.

Diversification Strategy – this is a strategy which takes the organisation away from its current markets and products. Diversification may be related or unrelated.

Referring again to her notes, Sarah found that she already had the information needed to consider these options.

Consolidation and market penetration strategy outcome

In the market circumstances facing MEL (new entrants coming into the motorsport components market and the long-term decline of traditional motorsport as the automotive sector moves to wholly electrical), this strategy seemed unlikely to offer success and growth for the future. Additionally, there was the important point that as things stood for MEL at present it appeared that overall service performance was falling away from meeting the critical success factors and this would need to be, at least, corrected.

New-product development strategy

New-product development based on existing competencies offered lower risk and lower cost opportunities whereas in the case of seeking to develop new competencies, it is quite likely that new competitors in the market already possess the new critical success factors now required and hence are already achieving success in the market. As MEL is currently performing below market expectations and the existing motorsport market is mature and moving into decline, there seemed to be little hope for success in a new-product development strategy.

Market development strategy

The growing electric vehicle (EV) segment of motorsport seemed to be a previously unserved segment and new uses of the existing product seemed to be the identified opportunities in wind energy and nuclear energy. The alternative of expanding into new geographies internationally seemed unlikely to be successful in the mature to declining traditional motorsport sector but could work in the EV segment in the future on the basis of success having been achieved domestically. International expansion into the much larger defence, offshore oil, and wind and nuclear energy markets might prove possible. However, MEL had not operated internationally in any significant way before, and so there would certainly be a need to create new competencies even if the operations were based purely on exports.

Diversification strategy

Unrelated diversification is always expensive and highly risky and hence most unlikely to be appropriate for MEL.

To integrate vertically did not appear possible given the nature of the supply chain of which MEL is part, MEL's suppliers are manufacturers of special steels already operating internationally on a large scale and MEL's customers are the end users of the high-performance fixings MEL makes.

It may be possible for MEL to integrate horizontally, there were other engineering-based, not fixings, component suppliers to the motorsport or defence or offshore sectors merging or allying with which might enable the sharing of resources and competencies, thus enhancing overall profitability by reducing total costs for the two companies combined.

Conclusion

The Ansoff analysis appears to indicate that successful strategies might exist around one or both of:

- *Selling existing products or services into expanding new markets, specifically EV motorsport, wind energy and nuclear energy.*
- *Identifying routes to allow consolidation or even market penetration in existing markets perhaps through potential acquisitions or potential alliances that would allow broader market access to the existing markets of traditional motorsport, defence, and offshore. Conceivably, there may be opportunities for horizontal integration that would yield resource sharing opportunities in the shared traditional motorsport, defence, and offshore markets.*

*Sarah noted that the TOWS analysis had suggested that there might be value in consider-
ing investments in areas such as wind and nuclear energy and EV components. This would
lessen the degree of focus built into MEL's strategic positioning. She felt that this reinforced
the apparent value of pursuing the second idea listed in the Ansoff analysis conclusion
earlier.*

Development methods

As well as thinking about what strategies might be pursued by MEL, Sarah knew that she
had to also consider how the company might be developed so as successfully to follow
them.

Box 7.3 How does Sarah do this?

A strategy is a plan of action. So, as well as what is to be done better to deliver our
goals, we have to think about how to do it. This is the question we consider here, what
methods of strategic development are available to us and which is most appropriate
in the circumstances?

Fundamentally, there are three approaches we might take:

- **Organic development –** building only on the resources we already have.
- **Inorganic, mergers and acquisitions** – joining our organisation with another
  forming a single entity by agreement or purchase.
- **Inorganic, joint developments and alliances of various sorts** – agreeing with other organisations to work together towards some joint end while remaining separate entities.

Sarah reviewed the details of her analysis of the MEL strategic situation in order to
think through the implications and opportunities presented by these three options.

Development methods outcomes

Organic development

The cash that MEL has available plus MEL's existing reputation for being successful
and well run should enable the successful opening of a market in the wind energy and
nuclear energy markets but perhaps most easily in the EV motorsport market. The
former are substantial markets served already by a wide range of existing suppliers
whereas the latter is new but set fair to grow rapidly and closely related to MEL's
existing activities.

Inorganic development

The Ansoff and TOWS analyses suggest that there is value in considering acquisitions or alliances. The cash that MEL has available might enable the former if the target was small and specialist and perhaps, therefore, itself in similar difficulties to MEL. The idea of alliances would depend on finding partners with the appropriate resource and competence fit to MEL; it would depend also on MEL's existing reputation for being successful and well run.

Conclusion

Either of these development methods might work, and the opportunities to do either need further detailed investigation, but in the case of either approach, it would seem to be required that steps be taken to stem the loss of reputation among key customers.

International strategy

Sarah then turned her attention to international strategy, noting that this would be entirely new for MEL apart from some experience shipping goods to the Motorsport customers when they were competing outside the UK. It seemed to Sarah unlikely that the financial strength of MEL was sufficient to enable making acquisitions internationally; however, there would seem to be a real opportunity to sell to motorsport teams based outside the UK. However, it was the case that all the teams already had existing suppliers for everything MEL does and would be unlikely to wish to switch, especially given the difficulties MEL is having with customer satisfaction in the UK. The UK having left the EU, would also be likely to put practical difficulties in the way of EU-based teams.

Conclusion

International strategy seemed to be something for the future, Sarah put it to one side for now.

The strategic options to be considered by MEL

Sarah was then able to list the following strategic options following the completion of her strategic analysis. She noted that in both cases, part 2 of the strategies would need to be done to stem existing failings even if nothing new was undertaken.

STRATEGY A

Part 1: Seek to sell existing products or services into new markets, specifically EV motorsport, wind energy and nuclear energy:

- *Conduct detailed market research in the EV motorsport, wind energy, and nuclear energy markets to develop an understanding of competitors, customers, products/services, and prices.*

- *Establish knowledge management processes to manage the decline in traditional automotive activity while retaining knowledge and key skills relevant to future markets.*

Part 2: Take steps to stem the loss of reputation among existing key customers by improving processes/skills to mitigate the risk that product delivered to the motorsport sector will be high-priced or poorer quality than that of competitors. The first steps towards this would include a detailed investigation and then a correction of the immediate causes of poor performance at the operational level. Also establish remedial recruitment to alleviate present concerns around staff age structure.

STRATEGY B

Part 1: Make acquisitions or form alliances that would yield resource-sharing opportunities in serving the existing markets of traditional motorsport, defence, and offshore:

- *Initiate international and UK search for potential acquisitions and alliance partners that can be delivered within the £1.5M available in cash.*

Part 2: Take steps to stem the loss of reputation among existing key customers by improving processes/skills to mitigate the risk that product delivered to the motorsport sector will be high-priced or poorer quality than that of competitors. The first steps towards this would include detailed investigation and then correction of the immediate causes of poor performance at the operational level. Also establish remedial recruitment to alleviate present concerns around staff age structure.

CHAPTER CASE

Generic strategies and online organisations

Porter's Generic Strategies date back to 1985. The world has changed a great deal since then, not least in purely online business activities. This case is intended to open up a discussion about whether the traditional approaches developed by Porter remain valid in the virtual world of the 21st century.

Research, published in 2019 and taking Amazon, eBay, and Google as cases for study, aimed to evaluate the extent to which Porter's Generic Strategies are useful in the context of purely online multinational firms.

The research concludes the following:

- *Amazon* has successfully implemented a cost leadership strategy to achieve a competitive advantage. To achieve this, Amazon has substantial warehousing facilities and handling capabilities.

- *eBay* has implemented differentiation as its generic strategy to achieve competitive advantage It has differentiated the firm by incorporating the PayPal payment system, which is prominent for its security, discounted rates, and network utility. eBay has differentiated its distribution channel by focusing on convenience, the security of transactions, and the speed of delivery. Trust and security are significant in customer loyalty.
- Through offering its unique products and services to different segments of customers, *Google* has pursued a differentiation strategy built around its huge technology infrastructure and has been able to set itself apart from its competitors through the uniqueness of its product and service offerings. Based on this strategy, Google can charge higher prices by matching customers' needs with specific products and services.

    Source: Rashidirad and Suleman, *Strategic Change.* 2019;28:167–176. Wiley

CASE DISCUSSION QUESTIONS

1. Relate each of the preceding examples to the factors involved in implementing the generic strategies chosen.

2. How can e-business firms implement Porter's generic strategy of focus to achieve and sustain competitive advantage?

NOTES

1   Porter, M. *Competitive Advantage: Creating and Sustaining Superior Performance*, New York: The Free Press, 1985

2   Faulkner, D. & Bowman, C. *The Essence of Competitive Strategy*, London: Prentice Hall, 1995

3   Ansoff, H.I. *Corporate Strategy*, London: Penguin, 1988

4   Whittington, R., Regnér, P., Angwin, D., Johnson, G. & Scholes, K. *Exploring Strategy*, 12th Edn, Harlow: Pearson, 2021

5   Bartlett, C.A. & Ghoshal, S. *Managing Across Borders; The Transnational Solution*, Boston, MA: The Harvard Business School Press, 1989

CHAPTER 8

Choosing between the strategic options

CHOICES TO BE MADE

It is more than likely that all this strategising will have left you with several possible strategies, each of which may well deliver your goals. The question then is how to choose between them. A choice must be made, and it must be done in a way which is systematic and can be explained to all stakeholders. This chapter offers such a methodology, the SAF[1] approach standing for **Suitability, Acceptability** and **Feasibility**. The basic idea is that we can score each of the contending strategic options against each of these criteria and thereby identify the one which best meets the whole set.

Suitability

The questions here are whether the strategy being assessed fits the situation and any other strategic decisions that have already been made, how well it fits, and how well it might exploit core competencies. These questions can be broken down into several sub-questions on suitability:

- The macro and competitive environments – Does the strategy fully exploit opportunities and avoid threats?
- Resources/competencies – Does the strategy fully capitalise on strengths and avoid or remedy weakness?
- Expectations – Does the strategy fully address the expectations of key stakeholders?
- Sustainability – Does the strategy offer a competitive advantage, does it contain elements of uniqueness, does it tend to make our resources more difficult to imitate or substitute, and can it readily be copied?
- Consistency – Is the strategy consistent with our other strategies, with our development direction choices and with our development method choices?

The results of asking these questions can be recorded in a table such as this for each of our options (here A, B, C, D, E). The scores, largely subjective, perhaps on a scale of 1 to 5, for poor to strongly suitable, can then be totalled to give an overall score for each against the suitability test and an overall position established from first to fifth, in this case.

DOI: 10.4324/9781003345398-8

	Environment	Resources	Expectations	Sustainability	Consistency	Total
A	1	5	3	3	2	14
B	5	2	5	3	4	19
C	4	3	4	2	4	17
D	2	4	2	4	3	15
E	3	3	2	3	3	14

Acceptability

Acceptability is concerned with expected performance outcomes – risks and returns.

It is important to bear in mind that many of the performance measures generally used were originally designed for discrete projects whereas strategic developments may not be so predictable and may not be so "neat and tidy":

- Financial tests – what is the impact on **Return on Capital Employed (ROCE)**, when will the investment make a return, using **payback** or discounted cash flow (**DCF**) tests, is the **cost/benefit analysis positive?**
- Risk – what is the downside of the strategy failing, and how likely is this; does the strategy impose significant financial risk (assessing impact on liquidity); and what is the **sensitivity** of the strategy to changing circumstances?
- Stakeholder response – what does the strategy do for the long-term cash generating capability of the business, and what is the attitude of key stakeholders to the changes proposed, using **stakeholder mapping**?
- Options foregone – if we chose this strategy, what else are we thereby choosing not to be able to do?

The results of asking these questions can be recorded in a table such as this for each of our options (here A, B, C, D, E). The scores, largely subjective, perhaps on a scale from 1 to 5, for poor to strongly acceptable, can then be totalled to give an overall score for each against the suitability test and an overall position established from first to fifth, in this case.

	Financial tests	Risk	Stakeholder response	Options foregone	Total
A	5	5	2	1	13
B	1	1	4	3	9
C	2	1	4	2	9
D	4	3	3	4	14
E	3	4	1	3	11

Feasibility

Feasibility is whether the strategy could work in practice. This test offers an emphasis on practical matters – Is there the resourcing and strategic capability to make the strategy real? We can measure this in two main ways:

- Affordability – both in totality and in terms of cash flow. To do this, use funds-flow forecasting in which outline cash-flow forecasts are constructed based on approximate expected income and costs as the strategy is developed from inception to full operation.
- Resourcing once implemented – This is a critical issue that is often overlooked, we need to think about the resources, systems, infrastructure, and so on that will be needed when the implementation stage of the strategy is complete. Will they be available in fact? For example, a hospital may buy the latest tech and build new wards, but if the key highly skilled staff are hard to get, the services may never be able to be provided to patients.

The results of asking these questions can be recorded in a table such as this for each of our options (here A, B, C, D, E). The scores, largely subjective, perhaps on a scale from 1 to 5, for poor to strongly feasible, can then be totalled to give an overall score for each against the suitability test and an overall position established from first to fifth, in this case.

	Affordability	Resourcing	Total
A	5	5	10
B	1	1	2
C	3	3	6
D	4	4	8
E	3	2	5

Evaluation of the overall position

The rankings achieved under each heading for each test, from the best, 5, to the worst, 1, in this case, are then brought together and an overall ranking established using a table such as this.

Strategic options	Suitability ranking	Acceptability ranking	Feasibility ranking	Overall Ranking
A	1	4	5	10
B	5	1	1	7

Strategic options	Suitability ranking	Acceptability ranking	Feasibility ranking	Overall Ranking
C	4	1	3	8
D	3	5	4	12 – first choice
E	1	3	2	6

The strategic option with the highest overall ranking is the one which is most likely to be most successful overall.

THE MEL CASE

Having assembled some strategic options Sarah had now to consider how to make a reasoned choice between them and what she should recommend to the Management Team of MEL.

Box 8.1 How did Sarah do this?

A choice must be made, and it must be done in a way which is systematic and can be explained to all stakeholders. This chapter offers such a methodology, the **SAF** approach (Whittington et al., 2020), standing for **Suitability, Acceptability** and **Feasibility**. The basic idea is that we can score each of the contending strategic options against each of these criteria and thereby identify the one which best meets the whole set.

Suitability

The questions here are whether the strategy being assessed fits the situation and any other strategic decisions that have already been made, how well it fits, and how well it might exploit core competencies. These questions can be broken down into several sub-questions on suitability.

Acceptability

This is concerned with expected performance outcomes from the strategies – that is the risks and returns. It is important to bear in mind that many of the performance measures used were originally designed for discrete projects and strategic developments may not be so predictable and "neat and tidy".

Feasibility

This is concerned with whether the strategy could work in practice. This test offers an emphasis on practical matters – Is there the resourcing and strategic capability to make the strategy real, or is it perhaps just a pipe dream?

Sarah reviewed each of these questions in turn, checking her thinking as seemed appropriate with colleagues in Accounts and Operations.

Suitability outcomes

Five tests are suggested by the theory:

1. The macro and competitive environments – Does the strategy fully exploit opportunities and avoid threats?
   - Neither Strategy A nor Strategy B does so fully but Strategy A is the better.
2. Resources/competencies – Does the strategy fully capitalise on strengths and avoid or remedy weakness?
   - Both Strategy A and Strategy B do this.
3. Expectations – Does the strategy fully address the expectations of key stakeholders?
   - Strategy A is more in line than Strategy B with the views of shareholders.
4. Sustainability – Does the strategy offer a competitive advantage, does it contain elements of uniqueness, does it tend to make our resources more difficult to imitate or substitute, and can it readily be copied?
   - Neither Strategy A nor Strategy B is particularly strong here, but it may be that B could enable the building of a combination of resources which offer some long-term competitive advantage.
5. Consistency – Is the strategy consistent with our other strategies, with our development direction choices and with our development method choices?
   - Both Strategy A and Strategy B are consistent.

	Environment	Resources	Expectations	Sustainability	Consistency	Total
A	2	2	2	1	2	9
B	1	2	1	2	2	8

Note: *Scale is 1 to 2 for poorly to strongly suitable.*

Acceptability

There are four areas of testing:

1. Financial tests

    •   Sarah met with Tim Jones and Jeff Castle to assess the financial impacts of the two strategies. The tables following show the headline figures they projected starting from the expected 2022 results. Their view was that Strategy A pays back more quickly and produces better ROCE more quickly. They noted also that their projections relating to the decline of the traditional motorsport market might easily prove overly optimistic. They had seen that the growth of electric vehicles (EVs) generally appeared to be accelerating. This also favoured Strategy A.

Key Projected Financial Data for Strategy A	2025 £M	2024 £M	2023 £M	2022 £M
Turnover	25	20	16	15
Profit (loss) before taxation	5	3.5	2	2.5
Profit margin	20%	18%	13%	17%
Net assets (liabilities)	7.2	7	6.1	6
Return on capital employed	70%	50%	33%	42%

Key Projected Financial Data for Strategy B	2025 £M	2024 £M	2023 £M	2022 £M
Turnover	22	19	16	15
Profit (loss) before taxation	5	3	1.5	2.5
Profit margin	23%	16%	9%	17%
Net assets (liabilities)	10	9.1	7.9	6
Return on capital employed	50%	33%	19%	42%

2. Risk – what is the downside of the strategy failing, and how likely is this; does the strategy impose significant financial risk (assessing impact on liquidity); and what is the **sensitivity** of the strategy to changing circumstances?

   • *Strategy A is an extension of what one might do simply to alleviate the current strategic situation to manage decline. Hence, the downside risk, while significant, is little worse than a policy of inaction. Strategy B is a risky option in terms of the difficulties inherent in acquisition and alliance formation; additionally it is at least partly dependent on the international traditional motorsport market known to be in decline while the defence and offshore markets are highly competitive.*

3. Stakeholder response – what does the strategy do for the long-term cash-generating capability of the business, and what is the attitude of key stakeholders to the changes proposed (using **stakeholder mapping**)?

   • The shareholders have said that they will actively support a strategy that seeks to ensure the best long-term success of MEL. As a strategy of organic development, Strategy A is perhaps more likely to command their support given that there is no risk of their control and influence being diluted.

4. Options foregone – if we chose this strategy, what else are we thereby choosing not to be able to do?

   • Given the situation and limited resources available the main options foregone by Strategy A are around focusing on managed decline in line with the traditional motorsport market. This would not command the support of the shareholders. Strategy B foregoes the option to develop the new markets identified in Strategy A; given the decline of traditional motorsport and the highly competitive nature of the defence and offshore markets, this is a more serious negative.

	Financial Tests	Risk	Stakeholder Response	Options Foregone	Total
A	2	2	2	2	8
B	1	1	1	1	4

Note: Scale is 1 to 2 for poorly to strongly suitable.

Feasibility

There are two tests:

1. Affordability, both in totality and in terms of cash flow. To do this, Sarah used funds flow forecasting in which outline cash flow forecasts are constructed based on the approximate expected income and costs as the strategy is developed from inception to full operation. The following cash flow forecasts were prepared by Sarah, Tim, and Jeff.

Projected Cash Flow for Strategy A	2025 £M	2024 £M	2023 £M	2022 £M
Cash in (out) flow operational, activities	5	4	3	3.4
Taxation	–.298	–.209	–.119	–0.149
Capital expenditure & financial investments				
Equity dividends paid	–4	–3.5	–3	–3.5
Increase (decrease) cash & equivalent	**0.702**	**0.291**	**–0.119**	**–0.25**

Projected Cash Flow for Strategy B	2025 £M	2024 £M	2023 £M	2022 £M
Cash in (out) flow operational, activities	5.5	4	3	3.4
Taxation	–0.37	–.223	–0.112	–0.149
Capital expenditure & financial investments		–1.5	–.5	
Equity dividends paid	–4	–2.5	–2.5	–3.5
Increase (decrease) cash & equivalent	**1.13**	**–0.22**	**–0.112**	**–0.25**

Tim and Jeff noted that in the case of the projection for Strategy B, substantial and potentially unaffordable cash outflows are avoided by the dramatic reduction in dividends that would have a serious impact on shareholders' personal finances. The projection for Strategy A showed substantial cash inflows a year earlier than Strategy B, although not so high that eventually, dividends would be significantly impacted. On this basis, they felt sure that Strategy A was to be preferred.

2. Resourcing once implemented – This is a critical issue that is often overlooked, we need to think about the resources, systems, infrastructure, and so on that will be needed when the implementation stage of the strategy is complete. Will they be available in fact? *The key issue here is the worrying nature of the Human Resources situation in MEL. Correcting these features is in both Strategy A and Strategy B.*

	Affordability	Resourcing	Total
A	2	2	4
B	1	2	3

Note: *Scale is 1 to 2 for poorly to strongly suitable.*

Conclusion

The rankings achieved under each heading for each test, from best, 2, to worst, 1, in this case, are brought together and an overall ranking established using a table such as this.

Strategic Options	Suitability Ranking	Acceptability Ranking	Feasibility Ranking	Overall Ranking
A	2	2	2	Preferred
B	1	1	1	Second choice

Note: *Scale is 1 to 2 for poorly to strongly suitable.*

Overall, the choice falls on option A.

CHAPTER CASE

Garden Products Ltd

Garden Products Ltd (GPL) is a business manufacturing wooden garden products such as fencing, planters, simple furniture, and the like. It is in a commercial wood sawmill belonging to a large farm in the Kent countryside, GPL is wholly owned by the owners of the farm, Mr and Mrs Giles. The mill itself was established well over 100 years ago and is housed in one of the farm buildings. Tom Jones is the manager of GPL. There are 20 other GPL employees; two are supervisors and four are general workers. The remaining 14 employees are skilled and semi-skilled machine operators.

GPL has been making a small loss for a number of years, but this has not previously been a concern in the context of the larger scale operations of the farm as a whole, but the farm income is now under pressure, and GPL must start to pay its way. However, gross margins have been reducing each year, even though wages are low. Although the equipment that GPL uses is simple, it is old, and like the mill building itself, the costs of running it are more than would be the case for a modern sawmill of similar capacity. The reduction in gross margins is gradually worsening the commercial position of GPL year by year.

There has been little investment at the mill in recent years, and productivity has declined. There is an atmosphere of low and worsening staff morale, and there has been a growing level of sickness absence. This may have been made worse by the ageing workforce, but Tom felt that this was not the whole story, although he had been the manager for only 12 months and had been recruited from a modern sawmill most of the staff had worked at the farm, if not actually at the mill, their entire working lives now averaging 35 years. Tom had found it difficult to get new ideas accepted, and the thought that GPL must now make a profit seemed to have had little impact on the way that work was done.

The old mill building had been of an excellent design in 1890 and had been well built so that its basic fabric remained sound. However, access was difficult from the main road, and the facilities for storage of materials and finished goods were very limited other than in an open yard next to the dairy.

In order to try to improve productivity and help bring the mill into profit, Tom has invested £500,000 in two state-of-the-art laser-guided saws and two computerised turning and finishing machines. The new machinery will be delivered in just a few weeks, and he plans that it will be fully operational within 3 months. Tom will then be able to update the product range, offering more sophisticated and much higher margin garden and domestic products so as gradually to replace the existing range of rough and relatively unfinished "rustic" products. The new products would include items made from exotic and expensive imported wood largely replacing the use of local materials.

The area around the mill includes many villages where very large individual houses and estates of up-market medium-sized houses have been built in recent years. Although the recent economic difficulties have caused new building to slow it is generally anticipated that, within the next 5 years, up to 5000 new houses will have been built within 20 miles of the farm. Tom believes that the householders will constitute a ready market for his new products, and he plans to provide retail facilities at the mill.

Mr and Mrs Giles have told Tom that they have been happy to make this investment, but they expect to see the business starting to make an operating profit within 12 months. Unfortunately, the capital they have put into the mill recently and the downturn in farm income mean that there is now very little in reserve. They have no further family assets available, and there is little cash at the bank.

As a basis for thinking about what he must achieve over the next 12 months, Tom has constructed the following SWOT analysis.

STRENGTHS

- Tom regards himself as the only real strength of GPL.

WEAKNESSES

- Loss making and no longer able to look for financial support from the parent organisation.
- Ageing and inflexible workforce.
- Poor physical facilities.
- Current product range limited.

OPPORTUNITIES

- Large-scale construction of new houses locally.
- Local government support for rural business survival.

THREATS

- Competition from major branded do-it-yourself and garden centre multiples.
- Competition from online retailers.
- Parent organisation weakening.

Then, applying TOWS, Tom develops two possible strategies:

1. Seek to partner with the builder to provide him with the many metres of fencing he will need for his new houses and use the financial breathing space gained to develop the proposed new products and services.
2. Sell the new machinery unused, using his personal contacts in the industry to get the best deal and close the business while still able to do this in an orderly way.

Source: Authors' own practice

CASE DISCUSSION QUESTIONS

1. Apply the SAF strategic choice criteria to Tom's ideas. Which of the two would you choose?
2. What other strategies might you have considered?

NOTE

1 Whittington, R., Regnér, P., Angwin, D., Johnson, G. & Scholes, K. *Exploring Strategy*, 12th Edn, Harlow: Pearson, 2021

CHAPTER 9

Successfully implementing a strategy

NEXT STEPS

Deciding on a strategy is all very well and very challenging, but it is of no value if that strategy is not then successfully implemented.

This implementation step of the process is by far the most difficult. The strategic decision itself is by its very nature complex and thereby complicated to implement, but additionally, the context is uncertain and subject to continuous change. Even while the strategy we have developed with such care to accommodate the context as it was and as we thought it would develop is being implemented, then the real context is to some degree, perhaps quite large, different from what we expected.

Strategic decisions impact every part of our organisation and the relationships we have with partners, suppliers, customers, and other key stakeholders. They are designed to create changes in these relationships but probably not in all the relationships we have, presenting the additional problem that we may well need to protect some aspects of our organisation from the changes we ourselves are making.

Most important of all and creating the most difficulty and potential failure modes is the fact that strategic change will always require the people who work in the organisation to change what they do, how they do it, when they do it, and with whom they do it. On the whole, people do not want to change their everyday life unless they can see a very good reason to do so, and hence, it is likely that changes will be resisted, at least passively and likely actively.

So, we need to do a complex thing in an uncertain situation and subject to resisting forces. How?

Project management

Implementation planning will involve taking a **project management** approach – that is the planned **management of change**. Project management is an enormous subject and is not within the purview of this text, but in the outline, we can say that it involves the following key steps:[1]

1. Define the project
2. Build a plan

DOI: 10.4324/9781003345398-9

3. Agree the plan with key stakeholders
4. Communicate to all those involved in implementing the plan
5. Get the work done
6. Monitor progress and update the plan – as often as necessary

Defining the project requires us to clarify exactly what are the objectives of our proposed strategic change, checking that this is in line with the organisational **mission** as set out in the **strategy statement** (see Chapter 3).

Good clear objectives are often said to be best constructed in a **SMART** format, meaning Specific, Measurable, Achievable, Relevant, and Time-Bound. In writing our SMART objectives, we can check that they really are SMART by asking the following questions:

- Specific – Is the objective clear, precise, and unambiguous, for example "open up a new market for our goods in France?"
- Measurable – Does the objective say how success will be measured, for example "taking a 10% market share?"
- Achievable – Is the objective realistically achievable considering the timeframe, resources, and support that are available, for example because market research shows that the market is growing at 20% per annum?
- Relevant – Is the objective relevant to what the business and/or the team need to achieve and in support the achievement of the overall goals of the organisation, for example because the 10% share will generate the return on investment set by key stakeholders?
- Time-Bound – Has a specific date been agreed for when the objective should be completed, for example "by the end of calendar year 2023?"

We now have the essential starting point for building our implementation plan, but it is crucial to do this in the light of a clear process for managing the various changes to be made in the organisation and, more important, its people.

CHANGE MANAGEMENT

This also is a subject on which there is a very extensive theoretical literature; what follows here is a brief outline of some key points.

The first step is to consider what scale of change is being attempted and what therefore may be an appropriate style of change management. Scale in this sense refers, first, to the impact of the change on the organisation, is it a relatively minor realignment or is it wholly transformational, and, second, to the intended speed of the change from very gradual to immediate. Considering these two scales we might set out four possible types of change (adapted from Balogun and Hailey, 1999):

- Adaptation – a very gradual adjustment of the existing parts of the organisation to be able to do new things with existing resources and competences.

- Evolution – a very gradual development of all or most aspects of the organisation towards some totally different activities using new resources and competences.
- Reconstruction – an immediate reconstruction of the existing parts of the organisation to be able to do new things with existing resources and competencies.
- Revolution – an immediate transformation of all or most aspects of the organisation towards some totally different activities using new resources and competencies.

In general, people will be less comfortable if change is rapid and if change is large, so revolutionary change will create the most psychological discomfort, and adaptive change, the least. When the level of discomfort is high, it can be anticipated that the resistance to change will be high. In light of this, we can seek to choose one of several different styles of managing change:

- Education and communication – a slow process of gradual change that will minimise internal political and cultural difficulties.
- Participation and collaboration – a slow process of gradual change designed to persuade, involve, and, thereby, commit to change resistant political and cultural groups within the organisation.
- Focused participation and intervention – a faster version of the previous process focused on the areas where change is to be the most immediate and impactful and involve direct intervention by the Change Management Team in the design and delivery of specific local change.
- Direction – involves the issue of instructions to change enabled by the direct intervention of the Change Management Team in the design and delivery of the changes to be made both globally and locally.
- Coercion – involves the forced replacement of any resistance by transfer or redundancy and the Change Management Team designing and delivering of the changes to be made both globally and locally.

We have dealt so far with the impact on our planning of the timescale and the scope of the change, but there are a number of lesser, albeit often important, factors to consider:

- Preservation – the need to protect parts of the organisation from inadvertent changes caused by the changes undertaken elsewhere.
- Diversity – the need to consider how changes we make will have a different impact on parts of our organisation where other organisational cultures prevail.
- Capacity to change – the existence of the resources required to make the change real.
- Awareness of the need and existence of a readiness to change – at all levels and in all parts of the organisation.

Inherent in all of this is a realisation of the fundamental importance of people-related issues in the management of change. Changing other aspects of the organisation (e.g. buying new software or leasing new premises) is trivially easy compared with changing people and their relationships, attitudes, beliefs, motivations, vision, knowledge, skills, and the like. This is where leadership is crucial; people follow leaders, and leadership alone will determine success.

Key things for the leader to address in managing change will be the following:

- Communicating the need for change – acceptance of need will help a lot to overcome resistance to change.
- Communicating the practical changes and supporting adjustment processes – helping people to understand what is changing, why it is happening, and how they will be helped to change themselves to meet new requirements will be important in easing the process of change.
- Enabling effective feedback from those affected – it is crucial that the leader can understand how the changes are impacting people and how they feel about this.
- Resisting growth of the grapevine – it is crucial to know what is being thought and said, privately, about the change process and then to act to correct misunderstandings.
- Building a base of support for sustainable change – if people change superficially but do not actually accept and support the changes made then the new strategy will never operate well and is likely gradually to revert to the way things were done previously.

A TOOLKIT FOR CHANGE TO HELP ACHIEVE ALL THIS!

Force field analysis

Force field analysis is a simple idea formalised in the work of Kurt Lewin.[2] There are forces driving a change and other forces opposing that same change. Change occurs when the drivers for change collectively overcome the restraining forces. If we can identify and evaluate this set of opposing forces, then we can plan how to deal with them so as to enable the forces for change to exceed the restraining forces. We need to find a way in which the forces can be plotted and allocated relative values, thereby helping identify the current situation, what needs to be overcome, and where opportunities lie.

This is a simple idea, but it is not always easy to do in real life. Usually, a diagram or a tabulation is drawn to help visualise the whole array of forces.

Driver for Change	Evaluation	Restraining Force	Evaluation
Demand for better quality among key customers	+5	Shortage of suitably trained staff on labour market	−3
New process technology recently available seen as having high potential	+2	New machinery and software needed is expensive	−2

Driver for Change	Evaluation	Restraining Force	Evaluation
Market is growing	+3	Staff resistance to acquiring new skills	−4
		Limited internal funds	−1
Total force for change	**+10**		**−10**

Of course, many of the evaluations will be subjective, but some may be more clearly established, for example market growth rate. Either way, all should be expressed on a uniform scale, say +5 to −5 so that the overall situation can clearly be seen. In the preceding example, the forces seem to be in balance. Can we see any ways to increase any forces for change or decrease the restraining forces?

Commitment planning

It is perhaps an obvious thought, but clearly it will help our change process if stakeholders are more committed to help than otherwise. It is useful therefore to assess each stakeholder group to see where they stand. A tabulation such as the following is a practical methodology.

Stakeholder list	Relative Power	Would Actively Oppose	Would Not Actively Oppose	Would Help to Make the Change	Would Be a Leader of the Change
Division Heads	4			X	
Trade Unions	2	X			
Institutional shareholders	3		X		
Local community	1		X		
Customers	3			X	
Division A staff	2	X			
Division B staff	1		X		
Etc.					

This sort of systematic approach enables thinking about how each of the stakeholder groups might be approached to ease the process of change. For example, we might not expect to be able to get the trades unions to help make a change take place, but we certainly could seek ways to move their attitude to one of allowing the change. Equally, given the internal power of the division heads, surely we would hope to be able to find ways to persuade them to join in leading the change?

Three phase model for change

Kurt Lewin goes on to suggest a methodology for delivering change usually known as the **Three Phase Model**. Lewin recognised that the key changes to be made and the only ones that really are difficult in the end are those around people and their attitudes:

- *Phase 1:* **Unfreeze** current attitudes – recognising the need to change, even if that need is disliked will enable a change to occur.
- *Phase 2:* **Move** to a new situation – the typical approach is to identify a series of steps which, taken together, will achieve the overall change. The first of these steps should be relatively small and easy to accomplish to offer early wins to be celebrated. In the case of each of the steps, it will be necessary to do the following:
  - Explore alternatives.
  - Identify specific obstacles to change.
  - Decide on a detailed change plan.
  - Implement the plan, paying special attention to people aspects.
  - Monitor progress and make corrections to details.
  - Celebrate success.
- *Phase 3:* **Refreeze** attitudes in the new situation – take steps to ensure that the changes achieved are sustainable and now represent the new working norms becoming part of the **organisational culture**.

It is always important to monitor ongoing performance; it is always mistaken to assume that a change once made will continue to operate well. An important part of enabling the new situation to be maintained is to demonstrate that the new situation is better for the organisation and employees, communicating success with good news stories.

Change agency

A relatively small change in a smaller organisation may perhaps be implementable by one change manager. If the change is substantial, as strategic change is typically, or the organisation is large or unusually diverse even though small, then the change manager will need help. The change manager will need eyes and ears and voices and hands in each of the parts of the organisation in which the change is happening. These assistants are usually called **change agents**. A change agent is anyone who has the commitment, skill, and power to stimulate, facilitate, and coordinate the change effort. They may be either external or internal. The success of any change effort depends heavily on the quality and workability of the relationship between the change agent, the change manager, and the key decision makers within the organisation. An important part of planning for the change is then to identify and recruit a change agent network using the following steps:

- Step 1: Identify your change agents asking the questions:

  - How does change successfully happen in this organisation?
  - Which parts of this organisation need to change?
  - Who in these parts has the necessary skills and commitment?

- Step 2: Engaging your change agents. Your chosen change agents may or may not yet be ready to influence and make the necessary changes to develop and offer local leadership.

  - Who and what will be most effective in gaining this change agent's support and interest?
  - How should you approach this person to involve them in the network? What information will be most compelling to them – for example the market research results, your organisation's business case for the strategic change, feedback from customers, and so on?

- Step 3: Mobilising your change agents to ensure that the rationale and approach for developing and embedding the change is visible throughout the organisation. Their role is to do the following:

  - Oversee the progress of the change and help facilitate the necessary actions each in their own locale.
  - Provide a link back to the change manager and the senior decision-making team on the progress being achieved.
  - Collectively take overall responsibility for the successful development and embedding of the change by delivering the necessary local changes.

A few thoughts on the overall management of the change process

As with any process, monitoring and control is essential. A change process cannot be unguided; else, it will certainly run off course. It is necessary to assess performance against the plan and be prepared to change the means and the route while maintaining focus on the fundamental aims of the process. Equally, it is important to avoid paralysis by over-control; there must be room for learning and emergent good practices, especially in response to changed circumstances. This is, of course, all a part of good leadership. Performance should be assessed at least in relation to the following:

- Approach to delivery of critical success factors.
- Achieving milestones.
- Adequacy of resource allocation.
- Future resource needs.
- Changes in external and internal environments.
- Feedback from change agents.

Successful implementation of strategic change requires clarity about the vision and the ability to lead people to change themselves.

THE MEL CASE

Now Sarah had to think through what the change management implications of this choice were if the Management Team accepted Sarah's conclusions.

Box 9.1 How did Sarah do this?

Key things for the leader to address in managing change will be the following:

- Communicating the need for change – acceptance of need will help a lot to overcome resistance to change.
- Communicating the practical changes and supporting adjustment processes – helping people understand what is actually changing, why it is happening, and how they will be helped to change themselves to meet new requirements will be really important in easing the process of change.
- Enabling effective feedback from those affected – it is crucial that the leader is able to understand how the changes are impacting people and how they feel about this.
- Resisting growth of the grapevine – it is crucial to know what is being thought and said, privately, about the change process and then to act to correct misunderstandings.
- Building a base of support for sustainable change – if people change superficially but do not actually accept and support the changes made then the new strategy will never operate well and is likely gradually to revert to the way things were done previously.

Sarah reviewed her notes of all her discussions with colleagues and thought long and hard about her own experiences as an employee of MEL. She took particular note of the views of the Management Team, the key stakeholders.

Applying the management of change toolkit outcome

Sarah started by constructing a force field diagram, as follows, so that she could understand and evaluate the relative size of the drivers for change and the restraining forces with which she would have to deal.

Driver for Change	Evaluation	Restraining Force	Evaluation
1. Loss of reputation among key customers and consequent impact on sales	+5	1. Shortage of suitable highly skilled staff in the UK labour market	−3
2. Gradual move away from traditional motorsport to electric vehicle–based motorsport	+2	2. Limited financial resources which are currently reducing as sales fall	−4
3. Aging workforce threatening loss of key skills and knowledge	+4	3. Mid-career staff resistance to acquiring new skills	−2
		4. Leadership Team and product designers lacking knowledge of the proposed new markets	−3
Total force for change	**+11**		**−12**

Sarah then asked herself whether she could see any ways to increase any drivers of change or decrease the restraining forces. She noted that the move from traditional automotive products to electric vehicle (EV) products was accelerating quickly across the automotive industry as a whole. She felt that she had to assume that this would apply also to motorsport. Equally, it was clear to her that loss of reputation, if not stemmed by swift action, would worsen to becoming irretrievable quite quickly. So, both Driver for Change 1 and Driver for Change 2 would increase in strength rapidly over time.

Turning to the restraining forces, she saw that swift action would reduce the impact of loss of sales on MEL's financial resources but resistance to developing new knowledge and skills and a lack of knowledge amongst key leaders and designers were more difficult to address.

Conclusion

Overall, she concluded that swift action, even if partial or to some extent misdirected, would be the right approach.

Sarah then moved on to assess each stakeholder group to see where they stood on the proposed strategy. She constructed a table as follows.

Stakeholder List	Relative Power	Would Actively Oppose	Would Not Actively Oppose	Would Help to Make the Change	Would Be a Leader of the Change
Senior Management Team/shareholders	5			X?	X?
Trade unions	2		X		
Local community	1		X		
Customers	4			X	
Current suppliers	3			X	

This seemed to indicate to Sarah that her strategic proposals were pushing at an open door, but she had to admit to herself that she was unsure about the Management Team in this context. It was clear to her that they wanted to take action to regenerate the success of MEL and to sustain it into the future, but at the same time, she doubted that their knowledge of the new markets would enable them actively to lead the process of change except as figureheads.

Conclusion

Sarah concluded that there would need to be a change management process organised in such a way as to take advantage of the potential of the Management Team to be figureheads while identifying change agents who either already had or could acquire the necessary knowledge of the new markets.

Thinking then of the change process itself Sarah applied the ideas of Lewin (1952) and the Three Phase Model in which it is recognised that the key changes to be made and the only ones that really are difficult in the end are those around people and their attitudes.

Phase 1: Unfreeze current attitudes – recognising the need to change, even if that need is disliked will enable a change to occur:

• Sarah thought it probable that staff at MEL, especially those in direct contact with customers, were well aware that things were not going well. It would be necessary to build on this, not only ensuring that this knowledge was widespread but also ensuring that staff realised that a plan had been formed to address the problem and that there was no obvious alternative other than more or less planned decline.

Phase 2: Move to a new situation – the typical approach is to identify a series of steps which, taken together, will achieve the overall change. The first of these steps should be relatively small and easy to accomplish to offer early wins to be celebrated.

- The chosen strategy was already constructed in the form of a series of steps. The first of these "detailed investigation and then correction of the immediate causes of poor performance at the operational level" was indeed a relatively small and obviously appropriate response to the drop in sales and loss of reputation.
- Sarah recognised that she would need to construct a detailed plan for the implementation of the whole strategy step by step. In the case of each of the steps it would be necessary for her to do the following:
  - Explore alternatives.
  - Identify specific obstacles to change.
  - Decide on a detailed change plan.
  - Implement the plan, paying special attention to people aspects.
  - Monitor progress and make corrections to details.
- It would also be necessary, she knew, to build confidence and motivation for further change by celebrating success in an ongoing and comprehensive campaign of staff communications. An important part of enabling the new situation to be maintained would be to demonstrate that the new situation was indeed better for the organisation and employees, communicating success to all through good news stories.

Phase 3: Refreeze attitudes in the new situation – take steps to ensure that the changes achieved are sustainable and now represent the new working norms becoming part of the **organisational culture**:

- The changes in staff and markets required by the implementation of the strategy would necessarily result in significant cultural change within MEL, but there would continue to be a large proportion of the staff who were part of the old culture so that refreezing the new working attitudes would be very necessary to ensure a maximum impact from the new strategy. The Senior Management Team might in this context be a specific problem to be dealt with.
- As with any process, monitoring and control would be essential. It will be necessary to assess performance against the plan. Equally, it would be important to avoid paralysis by over-control; Sarah knew that she must leave room for learning and emergent good practice, especially in response to changed circumstances as new staff and new markets have their impact on MEL.

Overall Conclusion

Sarah was now able to present her conclusions to the Senior Management Team.

She planned to ask for the immediate go-ahead for Strategy A. She would ask to be given the role of change manager and to be allowed to recruit a change agent from within each area of MEL. They would act under her control as local change managers implementing the agreed changes, following thorough local consultation and feeding back to Sarah on the progress they were making.

CHAPTER CASE

Change management in Denmark

In 2017, the Danish emergency management organisations were merged from 87 municipality-based organisations into 20 larger units, enabling substantial budget cuts. The overall challenge for the emergency management organisations was to plan and implement the merger on the rather short timescale of about 6 months. A research project followed the change management process.

It is often claimed that most change management does not produce the planned change but fails badly. Explanations for this high failure rate tend to point to resistance on behalf of the employees or the persistence of old organisational habits and practices. However, it is argued also that the failure to accomplish successful change lies with the 'one size fits all' approaches to change management. It is increasingly recognised that organisations are complex and dynamic systems and that change strategies accordingly must be flexible to achieve optimum fit with the conditions prevailing in the organisation undergoing change.

In the case of the Danish emergency management organisation, the main rationale for the change was regarded by all work groups as being budget cuts and having been caused by an external political decision. The change had a large impact on work practices, organisational values, and the identity of the employees. When asked how the changes influenced their identity or values, all work groups answered that their organisational pride was diminished, largely because they expected the budget cuts to influence the service they provided and the quality of their work negatively. The change constituted a profound psychological force within the organisation, referred to as a "forced marriage" by a representative of the management. The indicators were that the change would therefore be very difficult to implement successfully.

However, when asked how motivated they were to implement the change, most of the employees answered that they had accepted the change and were very motivated to take part in the change process. Considering the extent of the change and the predominant political and economic motive for the merger, this was quite remarkable. Even more surprising, the employees were more satisfied than dissatisfied with the political decision regarding the merger in the first place. The main reason given for this enthusiasm was that the merger promised potential benefits related to being part of a larger organisation. The employees looked forward to more cooperation, knowledge sharing, and the chance to undertake new assignments.

A success indeed, especially given the apparently difficult initial position. The employees perceive the changes as being both meaningful and acceptable, and they were very keen to take part in the intended actions, and the overall strategy of merging. How was this done?

The approach taken, despite the urgency, was of generating dialogue amongst the employees and with the Change Management Team. To evaluate the dialogue method and validate results, the employees were asked their opinions in an interactive survey. All participants voted that the dialogue, which was set up in the form of workshops, was good or very good. Most of the employees voted that this was a relevant method to achieve change in their organisation and regarded the subjects discussed as relevant or very relevant and believed the solutions found in the workshops were realistic and usable as a point of departure for working in the direction of durable solutions. There were no negative responses in any respect. The general feedback comments were that the method worked to get the participants involved, get their opinion heard, and get them to know each other.

Source; Lehmann, *Journal of Change Management*, 2017
vol. 17, no. 2, 138–154, Routledge

CASE DISCUSSION QUESTIONS

1. Assuming that the key stakeholders are the political decision makers, the senior management of the 20 new organisations, and the employees, construct a force field analysis.
2. Analyse the steps taken in the change by application of Lewin's Three Phase Model.

NOTES

1   Adapted from Reiss, G. *Project Management Demystified*, 3rd Edn, London: Taylor & Francis, 2007
2   Lewin, K. Frontiers in Group Dynamics: Concept, Method and Reality in Social Science; Equilibrium and Social Change, *Human Relations*, vol. 1, no. 1, 5–41 (1947)

CHAPTER 10

Worked case study example

BAMBURGH HOLIDAY HOLDINGS LTD

Bamburgh Holiday Holdings Ltd (BHHL) grew from a single family-owned hotel in the beautiful Northumbrian seaside village of Bamburgh. Through the second half of the 20th century and into the early years of the 21st century, it grew to encompass three other businesses in the same village, a café, a gift shop, and a caravan site just outside the village. Having achieved this size and range of services, it was now the dominant player in Bamburgh village itself and held a significant share of the market in a radius of 10 miles.

In early 2018, BHHL was acquired by the Holiday Hotel Group (see the following discussion for more information).

It is now early 2019. The group is reviewing strategy in light of its recent investments and, as part of this broader review, wishes to investigate BHHL and seek recommendations for its future development. The task has been given to Karla Garcia, who was recruited recently to the Holiday Hotel Group following her successful completion of an MBA at a prestigious European institution. Karla had a background in hotel management in the UK, France, and Spain.

Note: This case has been set before the onset of the COVID-19 pandemic in the UK in March 2020 to avoid the strategic analysis difficulties arising from such a major and unpredictable natural disaster.

OUTLINE OF THE BHHL BUSINESSES

- **The Bishop of Durham Inn** – the inn dates from the late 17th century during the period in which Lord Crew, Bishop of Durham, owned Bamburgh Castle. It has a bar, a lounge, a restaurant offering home-made specialties from north-east England, and 20 double bedrooms, all of which are en suite. There are also four family rooms, also en suite, which sleep four. The bar and restaurant are open to non-residents. The inn was last refurbished throughout in 2012, but all the public rooms were redecorated in 2019. It is rated 3 star and is the most expensive accommodation and restaurant in Bamburgh and its immediate environs. The majority of the customers are from the

DOI: 10.4324/9781003345398-10

UK, with the occasional international tourist, usually from the US, Canada, Australia, or New Zealand, and believed usually to be en route to or from Scotland.

- **The Cricket Pavilion Café/Bar** – located immediately below the castle walls and overlooking the village cricket ground to the front and with beach and sea views from the terrace at its rear, this café and bar is popular with locals and holidaymakers. It serves locally sourced organic food from 10:00 to 21:00 every day. Prices are set at around the average for Northumberland.
- **Bishop's Gifts** – this small gift shop is on the village's main street, a short walk from the inn. It offers locally sourced craftwork of all types.
- **Castle Farm Camping** – is located just outside the village with access from the main road. The farm offers a fixed and touring caravan and campsite and upmarket glamping in shepherd's huts. While the camping and caravanning offer is at around the average price for Northumberland, the glamping is distinctly expensive, comparable with ordinary hotel rooms elsewhere in the vicinity. There is a shop/café which, as well as camper's essentials, also provides frozen homemade meals. The majority of customers are from the UK, but a small proportion are from Europe, principally France and Holland.

OUTLINE OF THE HOLIDAY HOTEL GROUP AND THEIR PURCHASE OF BHHL

The group operates 30 boutique hotels (a type of hotel that feels small, intimate, and quaint and stays true to its local culture) aimed at touring/short-stay and weekend holidaymakers around England, Scotland, and Wales. All the hotels are in recognised areas of natural beauty which enjoy good tourist traffic all year-around. Each hotel is run by a manager who lives locally. All the hotels in the group are listed as 3 or 4 star and regarded as being at the luxurious end of the tourist market. The group has always been keen to invest in its properties to ensure that they retain this reputation, and it encourages the hotel managers, through profit-sharing incentives (each hotel is a profit centre), to be intrapreneurial in their approach.

BHHL OPERATIONAL DATA

The following tables set out the operational results (pre-tax) for 2016 to 2018.

Notes:

The value-added tax (VAT) has been excluded from these data.
BHHL owns all the properties from which it trades without mortgage.
BHHL has no debt.

The Bishop of Durham Inn

VAT Excluded	2016	2017	2018
Average occupancy rate	80%	75%	65%
Rooms revenue	£700K	£656K	£569K
Restaurant and bar revenues	£200K	£210K	£240K
Housekeeping costs	£100K	£102K	£104K
Building maintenance costs	£10K	£11K	£30K
Administration and management costs	£50K	£51K	£52K
Restaurant and bar purchases	£30K	£33K	£40K
Kitchen, restaurant, and bar costs	£70K	£77K	£84K

The Cricket Pavilion Café/Bar

VAT excluded	2016	2017	2018
Café/bar revenues	£66K	£68K	£69K
Building maintenance costs	£2k	£2k	£3k
Administration and management costs	£12k	£13K	£14K
Café/bar purchases	£10K	£11K	£12K
Kitchen and café/bar costs	£20K	£22K	£22K

Bishop's Gifts

VAT excluded	2016	2017	2018
Sales	£200K	£210K	£220K
Cost of sales	£66K	£70K	£72K
Building maintenance costs	£3k	£4k	£5k
Sales, administration, and management costs	£60K	£65K	£65K

Castle Farm Camping

VAT excluded	2016	2017	2018
Average occupancy rate	75%	75%	80%
Campsite revenue	£50K	£55K	£60K
Shop sales	£30K	£35K	£37K
Shop, cost of sales	£10K	£12K	£13K
Site maintenance costs	£2K	£2K	£2K
Sales, administration, and management costs	£10k	£12Kk	£13K

Initiating the project

Karla's first step was to discuss the project terms of reference with the Strategy Director of HHG to clarify the group's wishes as the owners of BHHL.

Conclusion

HHG have made a significant investment in BHHL; they wish to be advised how best BHHL might be developed in relation to its existing strategic position and in terms of contributing to the overall corporate success of HHG. The Strategy Director noted that BHHL operated wholly in the same sector as HHG but included several types of business which were currently not to be found in other parts of HHG. Should those businesses be retained or divested?

Review of BHHL resources – Chapter 4

As set out in Chapter 3, the first step in the project was to conduct a detailed review of the resources available to BHHL.

Box 10.1 How was this done?

To help review the BHHL resources, Karla held a meeting with the BHHL Company Secretary, who also took responsibility for Human Resources, Finance, and Administration. As a preliminary step, he produced a list of resources. This was used to evaluate BHHL's resources by asking these two questions (see Chapter 4):

1. **How much of the resource is really available, and is it of a suitable quality/condition?** – for example assets on an asset register may be

semi-obsolete, staff may be under-motivated and overworked, factories and equipment may be ill maintained, and so on.

2. **Is it unique/providing a competitive advantage?** – Cutting-edge machinery will soon be copied, patents will expire, employee specialist knowledge will become dated – most of what is unique now will be a threshold or indeed, useless in the future.

Resources audit – outcome

- Physical Resources
    - BHHL owns outright all the properties from which it trades.
    - Bedrooms in the inn were refurbished in 2012, and all the public rooms were redecorated in 2019.
    - The café/bar was refurbished last in 2015 and the gift shop in 2013.
    - A range of IT and related equipment, mostly point of sale, leased.
    - Three fixed caravans to let and facilities for 10 touring caravans and 10 family-size tents as well as 3 "shepherd's huts"– style glamping facilities on the campsite. The three fixed caravans are approaching the end of their life, but the shepherd's huts were purchased in 2018 and are regarded as having a life of at least 10 years.
- Human Resources
    - 20.5 full-time equivalent staff including
        - Administration – 4 full-time equivalents, the Company Secretary has a part-time assistant/bookkeeper, the inn has a night porter and a receptionist; the 3 other units have a part-time bookkeeper each.
        - Kitchen staff – 2.5 full-time equivalents, the inn has a chef and a sous chef who also supply the café/bar, where there is also a part-time sous chef.
        - Serving staff – 6 full-time equivalents, a barman at the inn and one at the café/bar, and 8 part-time waitresses at the inn's restaurant and the café/bar.
        - Cleaning staff, 4 full full-time equivalents, the inn is cleaned by a team of 8 part-time cleaners who also have responsibility for the café/bar.
        - Management – 4, the Management Team is headed by the Company Secretary, there is a hotel manager (also responsible for the campsite) and a restaurant/bar manager at the inn (also responsible for the café/bar) and a shop manager at Bishop's Gifts. There is no marketing or sales function as such.
- Financial Resources
    - Cash at bank £0.25M.
    - Significant asset base.
    - No debt.
- Intellectual Resources
    - The reputation of the Bishop of Durham Inn and of Bambrough as a quality holiday destination.

Conclusion

None of these resources appeared to be unique in general terms. Additionally, several areas of concern were observed:

1. The inn is well maintained, but the rooms may be becoming tired and rather dated in design and layout compared with more recently established or refurbished 3-star hotels.
2. Both the café/bar and the shop are likely to need refurbishment in the near future.
3. The fixed caravans at the campsite need to be replaced.
4. Although the staff of BHHL is not huge, the local labour market is rather limited in scope, and there are many competing businesses of a similar nature across Northumberland.
5. The complete lack of sales and marketing expertise.

Competencies

Following the overall project outline set out in Chapter 3, we need next to ask what competencies are built on these resources and then evaluate them to see whether any qualify as core competencies which we might expect to yield a competitive advantage.

Box 10.2 How was this done?

Discussions with the Company Secretary were then broadened by Karla to include the rest of the BHHL Management Team who were formed into an ongoing focus group to act as a sounding board for developing the strategic project.

Having discovered and evaluated the resources BHHL had, Karla wished to discover what might be the bases of BHHL's strategic capability. Were there:

-   **Threshold resources**, that is those that we absolutely need to operate?
-   **Unique resources**, that is that are better than our competitors and are difficult for them to imitate?

Does this result in us having:

-   **Threshold competencies** enabling us to do the basics demanded by the market?
-   **Core competencies** that are better than our competitors and are difficult to imitate and create products or services that are especially valued by customers?

Conclusion

Karla was assured that, in the context of the immediate environs of Bambrough, the resources of BHHL were unique when taken as a whole. However, each resource taken individually appeared to be little more than a threshold resource, and some of these resources were becoming rather worn. What might be the core competence built on this unique overall set of resources? Perhaps, the ability to provide a complete, comfortable, high-quality holiday or short stay but ultimately relying on the attractions of the location in competition with other similar destinations in North-East England. However, Karla noted also that the business had no social media presence and that marketing and sales activity was confined to traditional advertising and support from "Visit Northumberland" the County website.

Box 10.3 How was this done?

VRIO test

Value – Does this competence allow us

- To take advantage of **opportunities** and neutralise **threats?**
- Provide value to customers *but at a cost* to us that still allows us to make an acceptable return?

Rarity – Is this competency

- Possessed uniquely by one organisation or only by a few others?
- Is it rare on other than a temporary basis?

Inimitability – Is this a competency

- Which competitors will find difficult and costly to imitate, obtain, or substitute for?
- Is this difficulty sustainable because it is not built on unique resources, for example key people can leave or key systems can be acquired?

Organisational support – Is this a competency

- Which the organisation is well organised to support?
- For which the organisation has appropriate processes and systems?

Looking at this from the point of view of the VRIO evaluation tool, Karla concluded:

- **Value** – *was being provided to customers but that this value might be increasingly focused on the restaurant, the café, and aspects of the campsite rather than the accommodation at the inn as would be the norm for HHG.*
- **Rarity** – *the complete set of resources and the overall competence built from them is rare in the local context but that this might well be temporary were a new competitor to enter the market.*
- **Inimitability** – *it would be costly to build a competing hotel and set of facilities in the area, but it is doubtless not inimitable.*
- **Organisational Support** – *BHHL is well organised and appears, on the basis of its long-term success and growth to have appropriate systems for the activities it undertakes – on the other hand, these activities seemed, to Karla, incomplete.*

The result of Karla's VRIO test is then as follows:

Value	Rarity	Inimitability	Organisational Support	Evaluation
No		Yes or No		This creates a **competitive disadvantage**.
	Yes or No		No	This creates a **competitive disadvantage**.
Yes		No	Yes	This creates **competitive parity**.
Yes	Yes	No	Yes	This creates a **temporary competitive advantage**.
Yes	Yes	Yes	Yes	This creates a **sustained competitive advantage**.

Conclusion

There is a temporary competitive advantage in the current situation in the Bamburgh region. However, there is no certain basis for a sustainable competitive advantage.

Performance

Karla had noted various concerns about resources and that performance appeared to be declining in terms of inn room occupancy. The concerns about the resources might well, she thought, lead to a worsening of this performance, and the same problem might begin to arise in the campsite. Karla consulted colleagues at HHG and reviewed industry-level information about hotel occupancy (e.g. using www.visitbritain.org/accommodation-oc-cupancy-latest-results). She saw that occupancy rates at the inn had been good in 2016, but the decline in recent years was a worrying trend of falling behind improving industry norms.

The external context – Chapter 5

Karla knew that before she started to think about the external context of BHHL, she must clarify her definition of the industry of which BHHL and HHG are a part.

Box 10.4 How was this done?

Karla applied the Abell model which suggests that we define our industry in terms of three dimensions and in order to get the answers to these clear in her mind she spoke with the HHG Head of Marketing. She asked three questions: who are the customers, what are the customer's needs, and how are the needs being satisfied?

Industry definition outcome

- Customers
  - Short-stay holidaymakers
  - Weekly stay self-catering holidaymakers (the fixed caravan and glamping rentals)
- Customer's needs (inn and camping)
  - High level of room and public room equipment
  - Comfort
  - Cleanliness
  - Breakfast
  - Evening meals
  - Excellent holiday location
- Customer's needs (gift shop and café/bar)
  - Range of affordable quality gifts
  - Affordable quality daytime refreshment
- How are the customer's needs being satisfied?
  - 3-star-plus hotel facilities
  - Facilities that have been recently updated
  - Well-trained kitchen, bar, and serving staff
  - Cleanliness at highest level
  - Excellent service all round

Now Karla moved on to investigate the structure of this industry.

Box 10.5 How did Karla do this?

To address these questions, Karla talked further with HHG Head of Marketing They applied the ideas in Porter's 5 Forces; if these forces are large, then the industry will be very competitive and the opportunity to make good profits will be limited.

The forces are the following:

- Threat of New Entrants – we can evaluate this threat by considering the problems a new organisation might face on seeking to join the industry.
- Threat of Substitute Products – we can evaluate this threat in terms of our assessment of the degree to which the customer would have to take on additional costs, possibly one-off, to switch to the substitute.
- Power of Buyers – evaluation of this is often made in terms of the relative size of the buyers and producers or the relative number of buyers in the market and the number of producers in the market.
- Power of Suppliers – evaluation of this factor is the inverse of the points made in relation to the power of the buyer.
- Competitive Rivalry –we evaluate this by looking at the structure of the industry; for example are there many similarly sized organisations making up the industry, and is there low brand loyalty? These situations will tend to create severe price competition.

Karla needed also to consider the industry life cycle. Is the industry mature then market share can only be acquired at the expense of other members of the industry, or is the industry now in decline which further intensifies rivalry depending on the rate of decline and height of any exit barriers?

There was also the question of strategic groups in the industry, but given the focus of this project closely on the future of BHHL in its local market and the specific questions asked by HHG, Karla agreed with HHG's Head of Marketing that it was not necessary to pursue this question.

Porter's 5 Forces, industry life cycle, and strategic groups outcome

Karla and her colleagues concluded the following:

- The risk of significant new entrants was **low**, both in general and locally; however, it is possible for small competitors to enter the market quite easily, for example as B&Bs. Modern digital marketing made these a potentially significant challenge locally.

- Many substitutes existed for leisure spending in general and holiday spending in particular; this was a **high** risk factor.
- Supplier power was in general **low** – there were many suppliers in the market to supply hospitality businesses however local supply of specialities might become constrained.
- Buyer power was **medium to high** – there were very many other competing locations and hotels around the UK; however, individual customers were not generally able to negotiate price or service.
- Competitive rivalry was limited in Bamburgh, but there were a significant number of similar hotels and campsites within easy reach; this was judged to be a **medium to high** risk factor.

So far, as the industry life cycle went, they saw that this was a mature industry, essentially stable in terms of growth albeit depending overall on increasing appeal to foreign tourists to balance a decline of UK tourists over many years.

Conclusion

Overall, it was Karla's conclusion that if one focused on the local market within which BHHL competed directly, then there was a significant competitive challenge which could, relatively easily, be worsened by newcomers to the business. The HHG Head of Marketing pointed out that, more broadly, the industry, as a whole, remained reasonably attractive to an organisation such as HHG with its good geographical spread.

Critical Success Factors

The **critical success factors** are the things we need to have mastered to be a success in the industry. What these are was Karla's next question.

Box 10.6 How did Karla do this?

Critical success factors are built from two parts: first, the fundamental needs of the customers which must be met and, second, the ways in which competitive pressures drive the successful organisation we want to be to act. Karla's discussions with her colleagues from BHHL and HHG were all relevant here. She had asked each of them to give their views on this point.

CRITICAL SUCCESS FACTORS OUTCOME

She concluded that the consensus view was as follows:

1. Great holiday location.
2. Absolutely excellent service makes up for almost any failings.
3. Cleanliness.
4. Comfort.
5. Wide range of services.

Conclusion

The BHHL Company Secretary reported being quite concerned by the reduction in occupancy levels at the inn. But he also noted that covers at the inn restaurant and customer numbers at the café/bar were on the increase albeit gradually. The Head of Marketing for HHG had commented that, unfortunately, the inn did not have any method for acquiring customer feedback, unlike HHG, so it would be difficult to identify which of the critical success factors was not being met. But, he said, he was in no doubt that there was a significant shortfall, most likely, in his experience, attributable to an overall feeling of a lack of quality and value for money. Karla's own experience in hotels across several countries had already given her the same feeling.

PESTEL

Having thought her way through understanding the competitive environment around BHHL, Karla knew that she needed now to investigate the macro-environment.

Box 10.7 How this was done?

We need to ask what are the macro-economic factors which are now, or will in the future, affecting the industry we are analysing. We need to know which of these is the most important over time: how they will cause the industry to change over time and the size, impact, and probability of the changes taking place. This is done using the PESTEL framework to identify the key influences on our industry and assess for each its potential impact and the probability that it will have this impact in fact. We evaluate, subjectively, by

A. impact on some scale, for example +5 to −5, and
B. probability of occurrence over an appropriate timescale, for example 5 years.

> Then we calculate the assessed potential as opportunity (if +ve) or threat (if −ve) by calculating A × B.
>
> Karla approached this by reviewing relevant material in quality news sources such as *The Times*, *The Financial Times*, *The Economist*, BBC News, and the like. She then again brought together her focus group of BHHL managers to get their input on her ideas.

PESTEL OUTCOME

The consensus which emerged was as follows:

- Politics
  - It is anticipated that BREXIT will create significant problems for the hospitality industry around the loss of EU-origin staff not easily replaceable in the short term, clearly a significant negative factor assessed as highly like to occur (−ve).
  - BREXIT may also, over time, result in reduced tourism from the EU due to the hardening of the UK border. A negative factor but perhaps not as great as might be feared, especially for particularly unique locations such as Bambrough, but assessed as very likely to occur (−ve).
  - UK Government is pressing for the creation of a wide range of new economic and trading relations globally and with the new EU. These will take time to develop but could only be positive for inbound tourism, a relatively minor factor but important in the long term (+ve).
- Economics
  - BREXIT is likely to result in a temporary reduction in economic growth in the UK. It remains very unclear how this will play out, hence a minor negative factor overall (−ve).
- Social Change
  - No factors present themselves.
- Technological change
  - No factors present themselves.
- Environment
  - The national emphasis on defending the natural environment of the wilder and rural parts of the UK is important for a hotel business like BHHL. There may be the opportunity to develop a species of eco-tourism, a minor factor perhaps but potentially very important in the long term (+ve).
- Law
  - No factors present themselves.

Conclusion

At the time at which Karla was conducting this study, the impact of BREXIT remained a key unknown, but Karla and colleagues took the view that overall, it was likely rather more negative than positive. They were particularly concerned by the impact on the workforce of the hospitality industry.

The strategic position of BHHL – Chapter 6

Karla was now in a position to pull together an overview of the current strategic position of BHHL into a SWOT.

Box 10.8 How did Karla do this?

Working from all of the material she had collected together Karla asked herself what Strengths, Weaknesses, Opportunities and Threats she had identified:

- **Strengths** – internal organisational characteristics favourable to our meeting our goals (see Chapter 4).
- **Weaknesses** – internal organisational characteristics that will hinder or limit our reaching our goals (see Chapter 4).
- **Opportunities** – features in the macro and micro-environment that favour us if we can take advantage of them (see Chapter 5).
- **Threats** – features in the macro and micro-environment that will cause us to miss our goals if we cannot resist or avoid them (see Chapter 5).

SWOT outcome

- Strengths
  - Reasonably strong cash position and strong asset base.
  - Significant share of the local market across a range of tourist services.
- Weaknesses
  - Marketing and Sales arrangements very dated.
  - Occupancy rates in the inn below industry average and worsening.
- Opportunities
  - Potential growth of non-European origin tourism.
  - Potential growth of eco-tourism.
- Threats
  - Impact of BREXIT on the hospitality industry and its workforce in particular.
  - Impact of the growth of online B&B.

This SWOT was then used by Karla as the basis for thinking through possible strategies.

Box 10.9 How did Sarah do this?

Sarah set up a tabulation of pair comparisons of all the possible combinations of each of the S, W, O and T. She then again assembled her focus group of colleagues and with their help identified strategies (action plans) which could turn each of these pair comparisons to the best possible advantage:

- Seeking to use strengths to take advantage of opportunities and to defend against threats thus leading to enhanced competitive advantage overall.
- Seeking to identify how weaknesses might negate opportunities and create exposure to threats so that the weaknesses can be addressed in the most effective way overall and making our competitive advantage more sustainable.

Conclusion in the form of a TOWS analysis

	Strength 1 – Cash Position and Asset Base	Strength 2 – Share of the Local Market Across a Range of Tourist Services	Weakness 1 – Marketing and Sales Arrangements Dated	Weakness 2 – Occupancy Rates in the Inn Below Industry Average and Worsening
Opportunity 1 – growth of non-European origin tourism	Invest or acquire to enable offering of a complete package holiday		Recruit marketing and sales expertise in digital and social media marketing. Developing suitable in-house tools and partnerships to form a presence in the global tourist market.	Establish programme to improve customer service excellence focusing on a diverse international clientele
Opportunity 2 – growth of eco-tourism	Reposition all BHHL services to be fully eco friendly	Become dominant local first mover in offering of eco-tourism	Segment focus for the international marketing to be eco-tourism	Establish training programme focused on developing staff awareness of eco-tourism
Threat 1 – impact of BREXIT on labour market	Partner with local colleges of further education to set up hospitality courses	Likely to be preferred employer for those interested in the hospitality industry for employment	Select member of existing staff to undertake crash course in hospitality marketing to enable urgent remedial action	Likely to get worse before it gets better, will need to invest to support reduced revenue
Threat 2 – growth of online B&B	Purchase local property suitable for online B&B operations	Will assist marketing of online B&B units		

Strategic options – Chapter 7

From the TOWS, Karla has a wide set of practical ideas about what might be done, but she also wants to know what possible types of strategy may be relevant for her to look into.

Box 10.10 How does Karla do this?

There are two related ways of looking into the business strategies that may help BHHL to operate its existing business more effectively. These are **Porter's Generic Business Strategies** and the **strategy clock**. Both provide frameworks to guide our thinking. The former looks at the different ways in which we might generate competitive advantage and the latter looks at the different offers we might make to our customers in terms of their perception of value for money.

Porter offers four possible strategies derived from a study of the market being addressed (a special part of the market or the whole market) and the source of competitive advantage (seeking to offer something special that customers will pay more for or seeking to minimise our operating costs):

- Cost Leadership
- Differentiation
- Cost Focus
- Differentiation Focus

The strategy clock offers an alternative approach which is more focused on the customer, looking at the price they will have to pay and their perception of the added value they will achieve from the purchase, both compared with the offer of competitors. The clock suggests that there are 5 broad types of strategy:

- No Frills
- Low Price
- Hybrid
- Differentiation
- Focused Differentiation

Karla referred to her notes from discussions with the focus group, asking herself how she would describe the BHHL market and offer to customers using the frameworks of Porter and the strategy clock.

GENERIC STRATEGIES AND THE STRATEGY CLOCK OUTCOME

BHHL seems certainly to be following a differentiation focus strategy at present. It is focused on a very narrow part of the Northumberland holiday market, although it is also true to say that it offers a wider than normal range of services to that narrow market. Second, its prices are above average overall. The challenge seems to be whether it can maintain this differentiated position given the present and future difficulties it faces.

The strategy clock with its accent on customer perception of the added value they will achieve from the purchase reveals a worrying situation for BHHL (see Figure 10.1) as its position on the clock falls within the area called "failing strategies".

Conclusion

A firm differentiates its products from those of its competitors in a way that makes them appeal more to customers, yet it seems from the occupancy data that so far as the accommodation at the inn goes, customers are increasingly less likely to buy. Differentiation is achieved through quality and innovation combined with responsiveness to customers – but these seem to be areas in which BHHL needs to make improvements at the Inn.

A solution could be to reduce prices and improve quality towards a Hybrid strategy This would align prices and perceived added value but it is not perhaps easy to reduce unit income, at a time when income from rooms is falling, and at the same time enhance the product?

Ansoff's Matrix

Karla wanted also to consider whether BHHL should perhaps be looking at new products or perhaps at completely new markets for their products.

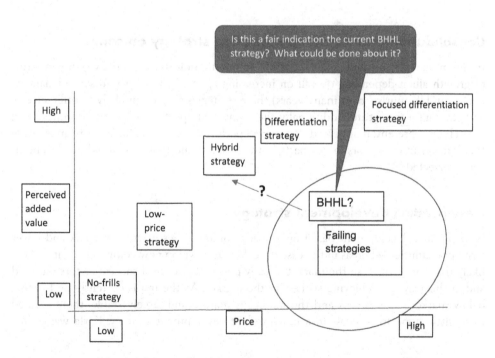

FIGURE 10.1 Application of the strategy clock to BHHL

Source: *Adapted from Faulkner and Bowman,* The Essence of Competitive Strategy, *Prentice Hall, 1995*

Box 10.12 How does Sarah do this?

She might look at the direction in which to develop our existing business beyond present limits using Ansoff's Matrix which offers 4 strategies.

Consolidation and Market Penetration Strategy – these involve protecting and strengthening the current position if consolidating and taking customers away from other suppliers if seeking to penetrate the market more deeply.

New-Product Development Strategy – this involves developing and delivering significantly modified or new products or services to existing markets. This can occur in two ways: it may be possible to use existing competences, typically identifying and following developing customer requirements, or develop new competencies, typically when the existing critical success factors no longer offer competitive advantage.

Market Development Strategy – this strategy seeks to offer existing products and services to new markets. These may be previously unserved segments or new uses of the existing product.

Diversification Strategy – this is a strategy which takes the organisation away from its current markets and products. Diversification may be related or unrelated.

Referring again to her notes, Karla found that she already had the information needed to consider these options.

Consolidation and market penetration strategy outcome

In the market circumstances facing BHHL (a mature industry, essentially stable in terms of growth albeit depending overall on increasing appeal to foreign tourists to balance a decline in UK tourists over many years) these strategies seemed unlikely to offer success and growth for the future. Additionally, there was the important point that as things stood for BHHL at present; it appeared that overall performance was falling away from meeting the critical success factors in key parts of the business and that this would need to be, at least, corrected.

New-product development strategy

New product development based on existing competencies offers lower risk and lower cost opportunities, whereas in the case of seeking to develop new competences, it is quite likely that competitors in the market already possess the critical success factors required and in this way are achieving success in the market. As the inn is currently performing below market expectations and the market is mature and largely stable, there seemed to be little hope for success in a new-product development strategy. Karla was aware, however, that the online B&B market was growing rather rapidly and that this could offer opportunities for product development.

Market development strategy

The growing international tourist market seemed to be a little served segment and new uses of the existing product seemed to be the identified opportunities in international and eco-tourism. It might also be argued that the ideas mentioned in the TOWS around developing a digitally accessed market constituted market development.

Diversification strategy

BHHL had a history of successful related diversification undertaken over many years and remaining within a very well-known local market. It was not obvious how this could be taken further or whether any such effort could be successful. Unrelated diversification is always expensive and highly risky and hence most unlikely to be appropriate for BHHL.

Conclusion

The Ansoff analysis appears to indicate that successful strategies might exist around one or more of the following:

- *Developing a new product around online B&B.*
- *Broadening the existing market addressed by developing modern online marketing.*
- *Developing a new market around non-European tourists.*
- *Developing a new market around eco-tourism.*

THE BHHL PORTFOLIO

A number of the ideas, beginning to form in Karla's thinking about TOWS and Ansoff, would require investment in the Inn, in B&B accommodation and in the overall BHHL marketing and sales infrastructure. Yet it was not clear to Karla that HHG would wish to make further investments in BHHL. To what extent might it be possible to find this investment internally? Karla recalled also that the HHG Strategy Director had said to her *"BHHL operated wholly in the same sector as HHG but included several types of business which were currently not to be found in other parts of HHG. Should those businesses be retained or divested?"* This seemed to offer one route to investing in the inn (the part of BHHL most obviously fitting with HHG). Karla planned to investigate this aspect by applying the idea of portfolio analysis.

Box 10.13 How was this done?

The most commonly used framework is the Boston Consulting Group or **BCG Matrix** also known as the Growth/Share matrixdescribed here. The vertical axis of the matrix is the rate of market growth. The horizontal axis is relative market share, that is the market share of the organisation being studied compared with that of its largest competitor. A particular point here is that a **problem child** may or may not become a **star** and that a **star** may or may not become a **cash cow**:

- **Star** – This strategic business unit (SBU) will need to spend heavily to gain market share; in a growing market all competitors are trying to get customers and will have to spend heavily. It is particularly important to invest in improvements that will ensure that a star becomes a cash cow rather than a dog as the rate of market growth slackens. This depends on maintaining market dominance against new entrants.
- **Cash Cow** – This SBU has a high market share in a mature market. Thus, stability exists and less expenditure is needed on marketing and other investments. Unit costs should also be low due to high levels of production. So, the cash cow is available as a provider of cash to finance other SBUs that need this. The cash cow is a very important element of the portfolio, its engine room, and should be managed conservatively and defended strongly.
- **Problem Child** – Little market share but a growing market, thus the SBU must invest heavily to gain market share. But will the investment pay off; brave decisions will be required either way – to invest or to disinvest?
- **Dog** – A cash drain on the organisation – this SBU has little market share and little possibility of growth as it is a mature market. The dog should be dropped but it may sometimes be possible to differentiate into a profitable niche.

Outcome of Karla's study of this topic

The UK holiday market is regarded as stable and mature. The rate of market growth is effectively zero. There are growing segments of the market, e.g., eco-tourism and international tourists visiting UK but even taken separately these do not constitute high levels of growth. Thus, the key factor to consider here is market share. When market share is high it can be expected that the opportunity to make profits is elevated beyond the average for the industry:

- The Bishop of Durham Inn – is the main hotel operating in its area and has the highest single market share in that market – it constitutes a **cash cow** therefore all else being equal, it should be able to contribute significant free cash flow to BHHL.

- **The Cricket Pavilion Café/Bar** – serves both holidaymakers and locals but in terms of market share for the services it offers it is roughly equal to several others (other cafes including on the nearby main road to Berwick, pubs, and the bar at the inn). Is this therefore a **dog**, or perhaps its role as the cricket pavilion gives it an important niche in local village life? However, the cricket season in Northumberland is rather short and the realistic size of such a niche rather small.
- **Bishop's Gifts** – the position of the gift shop is very similar to the Cricket Pavilion, sharing the market not only with a couple of other local shops but also the sale of gift items by cafes. Is this a **dog** also? No obvious niche presents itself.
- **Castle Farm Camping** – apart from the glamping, Castle Farm may also be a marginal **dog** as it also shares the market with a few, but basic, campsites on other local farms. However, does the glamping offer the basis of an opportunity to create a sustainable business that may itself become a cash cow?

Conclusion

Karla concluded that Bishop's Gifts and the Cricket Pavilion were both candidates for divesting but that Castle Farm Camping was not because of the opportunity for developments in glamping and because it seemed better than the other two to fit with HHG activities.

Development methods

As well as thinking about what strategies might be pursued by BHHL Karla knew that she had also to consider how the company might be developed so as successfully to follow them.

Box 10.14 How was this done?

A strategy is a plan of action. So, as well as what is to be done better to deliver our goals, we have to think about how to do it. These are the questions we consider here: what methods of strategic development are available to us, and which is most appropriate in the circumstances?

Fundamentally, there are three approaches we might take:

- **Organic development** – building only on the resources we already have.
- **Inorganic, mergers and acquisitions** – joining our organisation with another forming a single entity, by agreement or purchase.
- **Inorganic, joint developments and alliances of various sorts** – agreeing with other organisations to work together towards some joint end while remaining separate entities.

Karla reviewed the details of her analysis of the BHHL strategic situation in order to think through the implications and opportunities presented by these three options.

DEVELOPMENT METHODS OUTCOMES

Organic development

BHHL has a reasonably strong position in relation to cash available and a lack of current debt. Probably it would be possible to raise bank financing secured on its asset base. Alternatively, BHHL might seek to raise funds by selling off parts of the business that were not regarded as core and so not so important to its long-term future in HHG. These approaches to development of the inn and the campsite should certainly be considered. The TOWS analysis refers to a number of ideas for which this could be a sensible approach.

Inorganic development

The Ansoff and TOWS analyses suggest there is value in considering developing significant new marketing activities and focusing on growing international visitors and the eco-tourism segment. Like the idea of developing digital marketing for a new online B&B operation, these are areas of activity that are nearly completely new to BHHL. It may not be realistic to seek to recruit or develop existing staff to generate capabilities to meet this end. It might, however, be possible to form partnerships with organisations already having this experience, most likely, but not necessarily, within the broader HHG umbrella.

Conclusion

Either of these development methods might work and the opportunities to do either need further detailed investigation but, in any case, it would seem necessary to take steps at the inn to deal with the reducing level of occupancy.

The strategic options to be considered by BHHL

Karla was then able to list the following strategic options following the completion of her strategic analysis. Whatever else was decided, Karla felt that Strategy A was essential to be undertaken, and it is repeated therefore as Strategy B(i).

Strategy A – consolidate activities in the inn and campsite and ensure that customers are ultra-satisfied.

- *Refurbish rooms at the inn and the old caravans at the campsite and develop a service excellence push.*
- *Divest café and shop to focus on tourist accommodation, staff to be redeployed to remaining units; this is in line with HHG.*

Strategy B
  Strategy B(i)

- *Refurbish rooms at the inn and the old caravans at the campsite and develop a service excellence push.*

- *Divest café and shop to focus on tourist accommodation, staff to be redeployed to remaining units; this is in line with HHG.*

Strategy B(ii)

- *Develop existing staff and recruit to enable developing modern online marketing and so broadening the proportion of the existing market addressed.*
- *Develop a new market around non-European tourists.*
- *Develop a new market around eco-tourism.*
- *Developing a new product around online B&B including purchase and refurbishment of B&B facility.*
- *Develop glamping offer at campsite.*

Strategic choice – Chapter 8

Having assembled some strategic options, Karla had now to consider how to make a reasoned choice between them and what she should recommend to HHG.

Box 10.15 How did Karla do this?

A choice must be made, and it must be done in a way which is systematic and can be explained to all stakeholders. This chapter offers such a methodology, the **SAF** approach (Whittington et al, 2020) standing for **Suitability**, **Acceptability**, and **Feasibility**. The basic idea is that we can score each of the contending strategic options against each of these criteria and thereby identify the one which best meets the whole set.

Suitability

The question here is whether the strategy being assessed fits the situation and any other strategic decisions that have already been made, how well it fits and how well it might exploit core competencies. This question can be broken down into several sub-questions on suitability.

Acceptability

This is concerned with expected performance outcomes from the strategies – that is the risks and returns. It is important to bear in mind that many of the performance measures used were originally designed for discrete projects and strategic developments may not be so predictable and 'neat and tidy'.

Feasibility

This is concerned with whether the strategy could work in practice. This test offers an emphasis on practical matters – is there the resourcing and strategic capability to make the strategy real or is it perhaps just a pipe dream?

Karla reviewed each of these questions in turn checking her thinking as seemed appropriate with colleagues in Accounts and Operations.

Suitability outcomes

Five tests are suggested by the theory,

1. The macro and competitive environments – does the strategy fully exploit opportunities and avoid threats?
   - Strategy A – no.
   - Strategy B – addresses most opportunities and threats identified.
2. Resources/competences – does the strategy fully capitalise on strengths and avoid or remedy weakness?
   - Strategy A – addresses one weakness, arguably that which is most immediately important and utilises the financial strengths of BHHL.
   - Strategy B – fully addresses the weaknesses of BHHL and utilises the financial strengths of BHHL.
3. Expectations – does the strategy fully address the expectations of key stakeholders?
   - Strategy A – yes to some extent; it deals with the basic wish of HHG to integrate BHHL into HHG operations.
   - Strategy B – fully meets the expectations of HHG, integrating BHHL with their operations and developing it in such a way as to build on the investment they have made.
4. Sustainability – does the strategy offer a competitive advantage, does it contain elements of uniqueness, does it tend to make our resources more difficult to imitate or substitute, and can it readily be copied?
   - Neither Strategy A nor Strategy B is particularly strong here, but it may be that B could enable the building of a combination of resources which offer some long-term competitive advantage.
5. Consistency – is the strategy consistent with our other strategies, with our development direction choices, and with our development method choices?
   - Both Strategy A and Strategy B are consistent.

	Environment	Resources	Expectations	Sustainability	Consistency	Total
A	1	1	1	1	2	6
B	2	2	2	2	2	10

Note: *Scale is 1 to 2 for poorly to strongly suitable.*

Acceptability

There are four areas of testing:

1. Financial tests

   Karla met with her BHHL colleagues to assess the financial impacts of the two strategies. The following tables show the headline figures they projected starting from the expected 2019 results if no changes were made. Their view was that Strategy B was to be preferred in terms of improved overall results and in terms of utilisation of resources that have been enhanced by a focus on one main line of business.

The Bishop of Durham Inn

VAT Excluded	2019 Projected on Current Business Model	2019 Projected Strategy A	2019 Projected Strategy B	2020 Projected Strategy A	2020 Projected Strategy B
Average occupancy rate	65%	75%	80%	80%	85%
Rooms revenue	£570K	£657K	£700K	£700K	£744K
Restaurant and bar revenues	£250K	£290K	£308K	£308K	£327K
Housekeeping costs	£105K	£121K	£129K	£129K	£137K
Building maintenance costs	£12K	£13K	£13K	£14K	£14K
Administration and management costs	£53K	£63K	£83K	£63K	£83K
Restaurant and bar purchases	£42K	£48K	£52K	£52K	£55K
Kitchen, restaurant, and bar costs	£86K	£88K	£88K	£90K	£90K
Operating profit	£522K	£614K	£643K	£660K	£692K

The Cricket Pavilion Café/Bar

VAT Excluded	2019 Projected	2019 Projected Strategy A	2019 Projected Strategy B
Café/bar revenues	£66K	Business has been sold	
Building maintenance costs	£2k		
Administration and management costs	£12k		
Café/bar purchases	£10K		
Kitchen and café/bar costs	£20K		
Operating profit	£22K	0	

Bishop's Gifts

VAT Excluded	2019 Projected	2019 Projected Strategy A	2019 Projected Strategy B
Sales	£200K	Business has been sold	
Cost of sales	£66K		
Building maintenance costs	£3k		
Sales, administration, and management costs	£60K		
Operating profit	£71K	0	

Castle Farm Camping

VAT Excluded	2019 Projected	2019 Projected Strategy A	2019 Projected Strategy B	2020 Projected Strategy A	2020 Projected Strategy B
Average occupancy rate	75%	80%	85%	80%	85%
Campsite revenue	£50K	£53K	£60K	£54K	£70K
Shop sales	£30K	£32K	£34K	£33K	£35K
Shop, cost of sales	£10K	£11K	£12K	£11K	£12K
Site maintenance costs	£2K	£2K	£3K	£3K	£4K
Sales, administration, and management costs	£10k	£11k	£11K	£12k	£12K
Operating profit	£58K	£61K	£68K	£61K	£77K

BHHL projected overall results

VAT Excluded	2019 Projected	2019 Projected Strategy A	2019 Projected Strategy B	2020 Projected Strategy A	2020 Projected Strategy B
Operating profit	**£673K**	**£675K**	**£711K**	**£721K**	**£769K**

2. Risk – what is the downside of the strategy failing, and how likely is this; does the strategy impose significant financial risk (assessing impact on liquidity); and what is the **sensitivity** of the strategy to changing circumstances?

   - *Strategy A is an extension of what one might do simply to alleviate the current strategic situation in an attempt to arrest decline. Hence, the downside risk is a little worse than a policy of inaction, and there would appear to be little sensitivity to changing external circumstances.*
   - *Strategy B is a riskier option in terms of change management, that is the difficulties inherent in recruitment, retraining, acquiring new skills, and developing new markets and products for which there is no previous experience. There is some sensitivity to external circumstances here, for example unexpected difficulty selling the two businesses to be divested or BREXIT impacts on the economy or labour market being significantly worse than expected.*

3. Stakeholder response – what does the strategy do for the long-term cash-generating capability of the business, and what is the attitude of key stakeholders to the changes proposed?

   - *HHG, the owners, has indicated that it is seeking to make the most of its investment in BHHL and is open to recommendations that involve a significant change in BHHL if that were sensible.*
   - *Strategy B aligns well with the indications given by HHG and results in enhanced free cash flow from BHHL.*
   - *Strategy A on the other hand merely limits the risk that HHG's investment will prove to have been poor.*

4. Options foregone – if we chose this strategy, what else are we thereby choosing not to be able to do?

   - Strategy A mainly forgoes the opportunity to build on HHG's investment in a way which will build the overall value of BHHL to its owners.
   - Strategy B foregoes the option to build on BHHL as it stands to offer a package holiday deal to tourists. There are no other examples of this product type in this part of the UK, its success would appear unlikely.

	Financial Tests	Risk	Stakeholder Response	Options Foregone	Total
A	1	2	1	1	5
B	2	1	2	2	7

Note: *Scale is 1 to 2 for poorly to strongly suitable.*

Feasibility

There are two tests:

Affordability – both in totality and in terms of cash flow. To do this Karla used funds flow forecasting in which outline cash flow forecasts are constructed based on approximate expected income and costs as the strategy is developed from inception to full operation. The following cash flow forecasts were prepared by Karla and her colleagues:

Projected Cash Flow for Strategy A	2019 £K	2020 £K
Cash in (out) flow operational, activities	675	721
Cash in from divestment	300	0
Capital expenditure	–175	0
Increase (decrease) cash & equivalent	**800**	**721**

Projected Cash Flow for Strategy B	2019 £K	2020 £K
Cash in (out) flow operational, activities	711	769
Cash in from divestment	300	0
Capital expenditure	–600	
Increase (decrease) cash & equivalent	**411**	**769**

Karla noted that in the case of the projection for Strategy B, substantial and potentially unaffordable cash outflows were offset by the sale of the two units being divested but, importantly, depend on success without further investment from HHG on that sale. The projection for Strategy A showed substantial cash inflows in the first year, likewise dependent to some extent on the sale, but that Strategy B overtook Strategy A from year 2 and would do so even if the sale were delayed. On this basis, they felt sure that Strategy B was to be preferred but HHG would need to accept the risk of needing further to invest if the business sale took longer than was expected.

Resourcing once implemented – this is a critical issue that is often overlooked; we need to think about the resources, systems, infrastructures, and so on that will be needed when the implementation stage of the strategy is complete. Will they be available in fact? The key issues here are around the need to enhance service and recruit or retrain staff to enable this in both Strategy A and Strategy B. The latter also includes similar activities to enable the modernising and broadening of marketing operations. From this point of view, Strategy A is to be preferred.

	Affordability	Resourcing	Total
A	1	2	3
B	2	1	3

Note: *Scale is 1 to 2 for poorly to strongly suitable.*

Conclusion

The rankings achieved under each heading for each test, from best 2 to worst 1, in this case, are brought together and an overall ranking established using a table such as this.

Strategic Options	Suitability Ranking	Acceptability Ranking	Feasibility Ranking	Overall Ranking
A	1	1	1	Second choice
B	2	2	1	Preferred

Note: *Scale is 1 to 2 for poorly to strongly suitable*

Overall, the choice falls on option B

Implementation – Chapter 9

Now Karla had to think through what the change management implications of this choice were if HHG accepted her conclusions. She knew that HHG would expect her to have prepared her ideas about this so that implementation could be discussed.

Box 10.13 How was this done?

Key things for the leader to address in managing change will be the following:

- Communicating the need for change – acceptance of need will help a lot to overcome resistance to change.
- Communicating the practical changes and supporting adjustment processes – helping people to understand what is actually changing, why it is happening and how they will be helped to change themselves to meet new requirements will be really important in easing the process of change.

- Enabling effective feedback from those affected – it is crucial that the leader is able to understand how the changes are impacting people and how they feel about this.
- Resisting growth of the grapevine – it is crucial to know what is being thought and said, privately, about the change process and then to act to correct misunderstandings.
- Building a base of support for sustainable change – if people change superficially but do not actually accept and support the changes made then the new strategy will never operate well and is likely gradually to revert to the way things were done previously.

Karla reviewed her notes of all her discussions with colleagues.

APPLYING THE MANAGEMENT OF CHANGE TOOLKIT OUTCOME

Karla started by constructing a force field diagram, as follows, so that she could understand and evaluate the relative size of the drivers for change and the restraining forces with which she would have to deal.

Driver for Change	Evaluation	Restraining Force	Evaluation
1. Rapid reduction in average room occupancy at the inn	+4	1. Costs of refurbishment represent a significant proportion of income	−3
2. Need to refurbish rooms at the inn and camping equipment at the campsite	+3	2. Existing staff lack expertise in key areas and recruitment expected to be difficult post BREXIT	−4
3. Limited nature of BHHL marketing expertise and limited nature of the markets accessed	+4	3. Mid-career staff resistance to acquiring new skills and resistance to changing roles and workplaces	−2
4. Lack of congruence between BHHL activities and HHG norm	+1	4. Management Team lacking knowledge of the proposed new markets	−4
Total force for change	**+12**		**−13**

Karla then asked herself whether she could see any ways to increase any drivers of change or decrease the restraining forces. It was clear to her that the haemorrhaging of room occupancy, if not stemmed by swift action, would worsen to becoming irretrievable quite quickly. Equally, the condition of the rooms and the old caravans would also worsen rapidly if not dealt with. So, both Driver for Change 1 and Driver for Change 2 would increase in strength rapidly over time.

Turning to the restraining forces, the costs of refurbishment could be met from the proposed divestment of the café/bar and shop. The staff difficulties would seem to be much more difficult to ameliorate.

Conclusion

Overall, she concluded that swift action, the first part of Strategy B or Strategy A, would be the right approach in the short term while the more difficult staff resources and capabilities issues were tackled.

Karla felt that her strategic proposals were pushing at an open door, but she had to admit to herself that she was unsure about the BHHL Management Team in this context. It was clear to her that HHG wanted to take action to build on the investment in BHHL and sustain it into the future.

Conclusion

Karla concluded that there would need to be a change management process organised in such a way as to take advantage of HHG resources of expertise while identifying change agents in BHHL who either already had or could acquire the necessary skills and expertise.

Thinking then of the change process itself Karla applied the ideas of Lewin's (1952) Three Phase Model in which it is recognised that the key changes to be made and the only ones that really are difficult in the end are those around people and their attitudes.

Phase 1: Unfreeze current attitudes – recognising the need to change, even if that need is disliked, will enable a change to occur:

- Karla felt that the staff at the Inn, especially those in direct contact with customers staying there, understood things were not going too well. It would be necessary to build on this, ensuring that this knowledge was widespread, but also ensuring that staff realised that a plan had been formed to address the problem in a positive way.
- The staff at the shop and the café/bar would be more problematic. She anticipated that they would all be able to be redeployed to the inn and the campsite, at least in principle. But this would be a big wrench for some of them. It would be necessary to convince them that the changes made sense for their long-term future with BHHL and that BHHL would be a stronger organisation able to offer enhanced careers in the future.

Phase 2: Move to a new situation – the typical approach is to identify a series of steps which, taken together will achieve the overall change. The first of these steps should be relatively small and easy to accomplish to offer early wins to be celebrated.

- The chosen strategy was already constructed in the form of a series of steps. The first of these, *"Refurbish rooms at the inn and the old caravans at the campsite and develop a service excellence push"*, was indeed a relatively small and obviously appropriate response to the drop in room sales and the state of the old caravans.
- Karla recognised that she would need to construct a detailed plan for the implementation of the whole strategy step by step. In the case of each of the steps, it would be necessary for her to do the following:
- Explore alternatives.
- Identify specific obstacles to change.
- Decide on a detailed change plan.
- Implement the plan, paying special attention to people aspects.
- Monitor progress and make corrections to details.
- It would also be necessary, she knew, to build confidence and motivation for further change by celebrating success in an ongoing and comprehensive campaign of staff communications. An important part of enabling the new situation to be maintained would be to demonstrate that the new situation was indeed better for the organisation and employees, communicating success to all through good news stories. This would be especially important in the context of the proposed divestment and redeployment of staff.

Phase 3: Refreeze attitudes in the new situation – take steps to ensure that the changes achieved are sustainable and now represent the new working norms becoming part of the **organisational culture**:

- The changes in staff location, skills and organisational capabilities required by the implementation of the strategy would necessarily result in a significant cultural change within BHHL so that refreezing the new working attitudes would be very necessary to ensure a maximum impact from the new strategy.
- As with any process, monitoring and control would be essential. It would be necessary to assess performance against plan. Equally, it would be important to avoid paralysis by over-control; Karla knew that she must leave room for learning and emergent good practice, especially in relation to enhanced service excellence and the development of new marketing techniques and new markets.

OVERALL CONCLUSION

Karla was now able to present her conclusions to HHG.

She planned to ask for the immediate go ahead for Strategy B. She would ask to be given the role of change manager and to be allowed to recruit a change agent from within each area of BHHL. They would act under her control as local change managers, implementing the agreed-on changes, following thorough local consultation, and feeding back to Karla on the progress they were making.

Index

Note: *Italic* page references indicate figures, and shaded and boxed text.

Printed in the United States
by Baker & Taylor Publisher Services.

Printed in the United States
by Baker & Taylor Publisher Services